Routledge Revivals

Recording Women

First Published in 2000, *Recording Women* documents the work of three leading feminist theatre companies, Sphinx Theatre Company, Scarlett Theatre and Foresight Theatre, through a combination of interviews with theatre practitioners and detailed descriptions of productions in performance. Each of the six productions is innovative in content and style.

Scarlett Theatre's Paper Walls and Foresight Theatre's Boadicea: The Red-Bellied Queen employ a skillful mixture of text, music, physical performance, humour and seriousness to explore, respectively, domestic abuse and rape (of women and community). Scarlett Theatre's The Sisters and Sphinx's Voyage in the Dark adapt existing texts. The sisters is a ritualized re-enactment of Chekhov's Three Sisters in which only the female characters from the play appear. Voyage in the Dark uses film-noir-like theatrical effects and the insistent rhythms of the tango to evoke the rootlessness and sense of alienation that characterizes Jean Rhys's novel. Slap (Foursight Theatre) and Goliath (Sphinx) are both one woman shows. Slap, performed by Naomi Cooke, explores images of motherhood, including lesbian motherhood and the concept of virgin birth. Goliath, performed by Nicola McAuliffe, is a dramatization, by Bryony Lavery, of Beatrix Campbell's powerful study of the 1991 riots in Cardiff, Oxford and Tyneside. This is a must read for scholars and researchers of theatre studies.

Recording Women
A Documentation of Six Theatre Productions

Geraldine Cousin

First published in 2000
by Harwood Academic Publishers

This edition first published in 2024 by Routledge
4 Park Square, Milton Park, Abingdon, Oxon, OX14 4RN

and by Routledge
605 Third Avenue, New York, NY 10017

Routledge is an imprint of the Taylor & Francis Group, an informa business

© 2000 by OPA (Overseas Publishers Association) N.V. Published by license under the Harwood Academic Publishers Imprint, part of The Gordon & Breach publishing Group.

All rights reserved. No part of this book may be reprinted or reproduced or utilised in any form or by any electronic, mechanical, or other means, now known or hereafter invented, including photocopying and recording, or in any information storage or retrieval system, without permission in writing from the publishers.

Publisher's Note
The publisher has gone to great lengths to ensure the quality of this reprint but points out that some imperfections in the original copies may be apparent.

Disclaimer
The publisher has made every effort to trace copyright holders and welcomes correspondence from those they have been unable to contact.

A Library of Congress record exists under ISBN: 905755092X

ISBN: 978-1-032-86037-4 (hbk)
ISBN: 978-1-003-52100-6 (ebk)
ISBN: 978-1-032-86039-8 (pbk)

Book DOI 10.4324/9781003521006

RECORDING WOMEN

A Documentation of Six Theatre Productions

Geraldine Cousin
University of Warwick, Coventry, UK

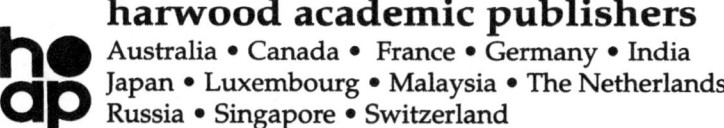

harwood academic publishers
Australia • Canada • France • Germany • India
Japan • Luxembourg • Malaysia • The Netherlands
Russia • Singapore • Switzerland

Copyright © 2000 by OPA (Overseas Publishers Association) N.V. Published by license under the Harwood Academic Publishers imprint, part of The Gordon and Breach Publishing Group.

All rights reserved.

No part of this book may be reproduced or utilized in any form or by any means, electronic or mechanical, including photocopying and recording, or by any information storage or retrieval system, without permission in writing from the publisher. Printed in Singapore.

Amsteldijk 166
1st Floor
1079 LH Amsterdam
The Netherlands

British Library Cataloguing in Publication Data
Cousin, Geraldine
   Recording women: a documentation of six theatre productions. –
(Contemporary theatre studies; v. 34)
   1. Feminist theatre   2. Feminist theatre – Production and direction –
Case studies   3. Theatrical companies
I. Title
792.9'5'082

ISBN 90-5755-092-X

Cover illustration: *The Sisters*, Scarlet Theatre Company, 1995. Gráinne Byrne as Olga, with Emma Bernard as Irena in the background. Photo: Sean Mooney.

For Erica, Jane, Dorinda and Julia

CONTENTS

Introduction to the series	ix
Acknowledgements	xi
List of Plates	xiii
Introduction	1
1. Scarlet Theatre	4
The Sisters	7
Paper Walls	37
2. Foursight Theatre	54
Boadicea: The Red-Bellied Queen	57
Slap	85
3. The Sphinx Theatre Company	102
Voyage in the Dark	107
Goliath	135
Afterword	156
Bibliography	162
Index	163

INTRODUCTION TO THE SERIES

Contemporary Theatre Studies is a book series of special interest to everyone involved in theatre. It consists of monographs on influential figures, studies of movements and ideas in theatre, as well as primary material consisting of theatre-related documents, performing editions of plays in English, and English translations of plays from various vital theatre traditions worldwide.

Franc Chamberlain

ACKNOWLEDGEMENTS

To everyone who gave so generously of their time and energies during the period of my research for this book, especially Gráinne and Marie (Scarlet Theatre), Kate, Sheena and Sue (Foursight Theatre), Alison and Sue (Sphinx), Katarzyna Deszcz and Bryony Lavery.

LIST OF PLATES

The Sisters, Scarlet Theatre Company, 1995. Linda Kerr Scott as Anfisa.	6
The Sisters, Scarlet Theatre Company, 1995. Gráinne Byrne as Olga, with Emma Bernard as Irena.	13
Linda Kerr Scott in *The Sisters*, Scarlet Theatre Company, 1995.	15
Gráinne Bryne as Olga and Jan Pearson as Natasha in *The Sisters*, Scarlet Theatre Company, 1995.	19
The Sisters, Scarlet Theatre Company, 1995. Gráinne Byrne as Olga, Helen Anderson as Masha and Emma Bernard as Irena.	21
The Sisters, Scarlet Theatre Company, 1995. Gráinne Byrne as Olga, Emma Bernard as Irena and Helen Anderson as Masha.	24
Paper Walls, Scarlet Theatre Company. Joyce Henderson as the Older Daughter with Christine Entwisle as the Younger Daughter.	36
Paper Walls, Scarlet Theatre Company, 1995 revival. Nicola Blackwell, Jane Guernier and Gráinne Byrne.	40
Paper Walls, Scarlet Theatre Company. Christine Entwisle, Jan Pearson and Joyce Henderson.	42
Joyce Henderson in *Paper Walls*, Scarlet Theatre Company.	42
Jan Pearson, Christine Entwisle and Joyce Henderson in *Paper Walls*, Scarlet Theatre Company.	44
Paper Walls, Scarlet Theatre Company, 1995 national tour. Nicola Blackwell, Gráinne Bryne and Jane Guernier.	47
Boadicea: The Red-Bellied Queen, Foursight Theatre Company. Stephanie Jacob as Boadicea, Sue Pendlebury as Voada, Katharine Ratcliff as Voddiccia and Simon Thorp as Marius.	56
Katharine Ratcliff in *Boadicea: The Red-Bellied Queen*, Foursight Theatre Company.	62
Boadicea: The Red-Bellied Queen, Foursight Theatre Company. Sue Pendlebury, Stephanie Jacob and Katharine Ratcliff.	64
Boadicea: The Red-Bellied Queen, Foursight Theatre Company. Simon Thorp, Stephanie Jacob, Sue Pendlebury and Katharine Ratcliff.	67
Boadicea: The Red-Bellied Queen, Foursight Theatre Company. Stephanie Jacob and Sue Pendlebury.	72
Boadicea: The Red-Bellied Queen, Foursight Theatre Company. Sue Pendlebury and Katharine Ratcliff.	73
Naomi Cooke in *Slap*, Foursight Theatre Company.	84
Sphinx Theatre Company's production of *Voyage in the Dark* by Jean Rhys, adapted by Joan Wiles, 1996. Ian Kirkby, Katrina Syran and Michael Vaughan.	106
Sphinx Theatre Company's production of *Voyage in the Dark*, 1996. Hazel Holder and Ian Kirkby.	111

xiv   *List of Plates*

Sphinx Theatre Company's production of *Voyage in the Dark*, 1996.
    Michael Vaughan and Katrina Syran.   114
Sphinx Theatre Company's production of *Voyage in the Dark*, 1996.
    Hazel Holder and Katrina Syran.   117
Sphinx Theatre Company's production of *Voyage in the Dark*, 1996.
    Ian Kirkby, Katrina Syran and Michael Vaughan.   121
Sphinx Theatre Company's production of *Voyage in the Dark*, 1996.
    Michael Vaughan, Katrina Syran and Ian Kirkby.   123
Sphinx Theatre Company's production of *Voyage in the Dark*, 1996.
    Anne White and Michael Vaughan.   127
Nichola McAuliffe in Sphinx Theatre Company's 1997 production of
    Goliath by Bryony Lavery, based on the book by Beatrix Campbell
    and directed by Annie Castledine.   134
Nichola McAuliffe in Sphinx Theatre Company's 1997 production
    of *Goliath*.   138
Nichola McAuliffe in Sphinx Theatre Company's 1997 production of *Goliath*.   142
Nichola McAuliffe in Sphinx Theatre Company's 1997 production of *Goliath*.   144

INTRODUCTION

This book grew out of a desire to record events that were trebly subject to the process of erasure. By their very nature these events – theatrical performances – were inherently ephemeral. In addition, the fact that they were performed (a) by small-scale touring companies, and (b) largely by women added to the likelihood of their being soon forgotten. I have called the book *Recording Women* because the majority of practitioners involved in the creation of the performances **were** women, and the central focus in the productions was to a large degree on the lives of women. This is not however to disregard the important contributions made by men, notably the male actors involved in *Voyage in the Dark* and *Boadicea: The Red-Bellied Queen*, the composers of original music (who were mostly men), Andrzej Sadowski who devised the text of *The Sisters* from Chekhov's *Three Sisters*, and, of course, Chekhov himself.

The six productions that form my subject matter were the work of three women-run theatre companies: Scarlet Theatre (originally the Scarlet Harlets) who are based in Barnet, north London, Foursight Theatre, based in Wolverhampton, and the Sphinx Theatre Company (formerly The Women's Theatre Group), based in south-east London near the Old Vic Theatre. My reasons for focusing on these three companies derive partly from personal interest, and partly from the fact that each has a proven track record for creating vibrant, innovative work. The Women's Theatre Group/ Sphinx has been established as a leading feminist company for over twenty years, the brief of the present Artistic Director, Sue Parrish, being 'to stage dramatic writing by women, either original plays or adaptations', which 'in some way' takes 'women forward'. Scarlet Theatre and Foursight Theatre (founded respectively in 1981 and 1987) are also well-established companies. Both, in their artistic policy statements, stress the importance they place on the collaborative nature of the work process. Both utilise a mixture of humour and seriousness, and blend physical performance style, music and text in the theatre pieces they create. Foursight Theatre are additionally characterised by their frequent use of women's biographies as source material. All three companies consciously engage with women-based issues, yet each creates work that is distinctive in style and texture.

In the case of each company I discuss two productions. Scarlet Theatre's *The Sisters*, an adaptation of Chekhov's play using only female characters (initially performed on 17 February 1995), is the first to be considered.

The Sisters toured in England (in 1995 and 1996), where performance venues included the Young Vic Studio (London, February-March 1995) and the Purcell Room (South Bank Centre, London, October 1996), and in Poland. Reviewing the production after seeing it at the Young Vic Studio, Kate Bassett wrote in *The Times* (6 March 1995), 'If the rest of the studio's season of experimental theatre is this good, the Young Vic is on to a winner.' The second production I discuss, *Paper Walls*, was also created by Scarlet Theatre. *Paper Walls*, which employed a mixture of striking visual images, humour, music and text to explore a story of domestic violence and abuse, opened on 18 February 1994 and toured intermittently until 1996, playing, among other venues, the Assembly Rooms during the 1995 Edinburgh Fringe Festival, and, in January 1996, the Purcell Room (South Bank Centre).

The two Scarlet productions are followed by two by Foursight Theatre: *Boadicea: The Red-Bellied Queen*, a feisty, physically powerful piece which skilfully combined tragic events with grotesque humour (initially performed at the Warwick Arts Centre Studio on 15 June 1995), and *Slap*, a one-woman show about three generations of Northern Irish women, which explored a range of attitudes to motherhood, including lesbian motherhood. *Slap* was first performed in Canada, where Foursight Theatre have a very high profile, in the summer of 1994.

The final two productions are by the Sphinx Theatre Company. *Voyage in the Dark* (based on Jean Rhys's 1934 novel about a white Dominican girl, alone and adrift in London) premièred at the Young Vic Studio on 9 January 1996. *Goliath* (based on Beatrix Campbell's compelling study of the 1991 riots in Cardiff, Oxford and Tyneside), was, like *Slap*, a one-woman show. It opened at the Gulbenkian Studio at the Newcastle Playhouse on 13 February 1997. Following a tour which included performances at the Traverse Theatre, Edinburgh, it played from 23 July to 16 August at the Bush Theatre, London. Among the many laudatory reviews was Bill Hagerty's comment in the *News of the World* (3 August 1997): 'Directed brilliantly by .... Annie Castledine', he wrote, 'Ms McAuliffe is breathtaking .... It's the performance of the year so far.'

The documentation of each production includes (italicised) comments by the practitioners involved in its creation, sometimes the director or writer, sometimes one or both of these figures plus the actors, and, in the case of *Boadicea*, also the composer and choreographer. For each production I have also provided an account of the piece in performance, and, in addition, a list of credits, tour dates, and a selection of quotes from reviews. The separate examinations of the six productions are succeeded by a brief consideration (in the Afterword) of their interrelation. Though the pieces were chosen as current examples of the companies' work, and not because they were expected to present similarities of theme, nevertheless there are interesting comparisons to be made, notably the exploration, in all the productions, of characters who attempt – with varying degrees of success – to extricate themselves from stagnant and imprisoning environments.

My aim throughout has been to preserve what could be preserved in book form of these six theatrical events – to provide traces, at least, of powerful, moving and, at times, very funny experiences. There is an anomaly in this, of course. Theatre (as I have already noted) is ephemeral. Playtexts, reviews, photographs, etc., survive, but the performances themselves are over; they had existence only in the present moment of theatre. One of the roles of the theatre academic however is, I think, to bear witness to what has been, and this is what I have tried to do. Appositely, the first production on which I focus, Scarlet Theatre's *The Sisters*, was vitally concerned with the nature of theatre: what this extraordinary, and yet quite ordinary, phenomenon is, its essential elements, its plasticity, its interconnection of past and present lives.

1
SCARLET THEATRE

Productions prior to *The Sisters* and *Paper Walls*

1981 – *We who were the Beautiful*
1982 – *Out of Bounds*
1983/84 – *Broken Circle*
1985 – *Toe on the Line*
1986 – *80 Day Soul*
1987 – *Appetite of the Heart*
1988/89 – *La Folie*
1990 – *(R) Age*
1991 – *Vows*
1992 – *Baby Baby*
1993 – *On Air*

Founded in 1981 as the Scarlet Harlets, the company changed its name to Scarlet Theatre in 1990. Scarlet Theatre is a national and international touring company, and has close links with Mandala Theatre (Krakow, Poland). In addition to its other areas of work, since 1993 the company has developed, in collaboration with the Education Department of the National Portrait Gallery, a new breed of performance that cross-fertilises art and theatre.

Artistic Policy

Scarlet Theatre:

Entertains, disturbs and provokes audiences by using humour as a vehicle for exposing profound human themes.

Deepens the audience's appreciation and understanding of theatre by facilitating an exchange of views, extending understanding, and providing opportunities for feedback on the Company's work.

Develops the language of theatre performance by exploring new ways of ensemble working, and of interpreting subjects, using a fusion of humour, tragedy, physical acting, text, powerful visual images and original music.

Forges new working relationships with organisations, international artists and funding partners to gain fresh insight and inspiration.

Fosters new talent by responding to, and developing initiatives for emerging artists through sharing skills and experience.

Enthuses, inspires and challenges female artists by providing them with opportunities to explore the boundaries of artform divisions.

Elevates the status of the older actress, especially in the area of devised physical work.

Tours challenging original theatre created from an all-female perspective but of relevance to everyone.

In pursuance of the fourth of these aims, Gráinne Byrne, the Artistic Director of Scarlet Theatre, invited the Polish director, Katarzyna Deszcz, to undertake a six-day workshop in September 1993, as part of Scarlet's European Directors' Season. As a result of this workshop, Gráinne extended a further invitation to Kasia, this time to direct a production with the company. Kasia agreed and chose to work on Chekhov's *Three Sisters* in a shortened and adapted form composed by her husband and fellow practitioner, Andrzej Sadowski. Kasia and Andrzej are co-founders of the Krakow-based Mandala Theatre.

The Sisters, Scarlet Theatre Company, 1995. Linda Kerr Scott as Anfisa. Directed by Katarzyna Deszcz, text composition by Andrzej Sadowski. Photo: Sheila Burnett

The Sisters

Credits

Direction	Katarzyna Deszcz
Text Composition and Scenography	Andrzej Sadowski
Design and Costumes	Sophia Lovell-Smith
Original music	Nigel Piper
Lighting Design	Jo Joelson

Cast Lists

Original team – 1995 National tour

Natasha: Jan Pearson
Masha: Helen Anderson
Irena: Emma Bernard
Olga: Gráinne Byrne
Anfisa: Linda Kerr Scott

July 1996 revival – Watermans and Polish tour

Natasha: Jan Pearson
Masha: Athena Constantine
Irena: Hailey Carmichael
Olga: Gráinne Byrne
Anfisa: Linda Kerr Scott

August 1996 – Fringe Festival (first two weeks)

Natasha: Jan Pearson
Masha: Athena Constantine
Irena: Hailey Carmichael
Olga: Gráinne Byrne
Anfisa: Linda Kerr Scott

August 1996 – Edinburgh Festival (third week), and October 1996, Purcell Room

Natasha: Jan Pearson
Masha: Athena Constantine
Irena: Emma Bernard
Olga: Gráinne Byrne
Anfisa: Linda Kerr Scott

Katarzyna Deszcz (director) on the ideas underpinning The Sisters

Building a theatre: *When Scarlet Theatre invited me to direct a production for them I immediately thought of Chekhov's* Three Sisters *which is one of the most interesting plays I know. It was always my intention to do an adaptation of the play because I don't see any point now in just taking a classical text and showing it on the stage, but I didn't realise to begin with that Scarlet Theatre is an all-women company, and, when I did, I wondered if the idea would work. The main characters though are women, and, after Andrzej and I had talked about it for a while, we decided that it would be very interesting to bring the five women from the play, minus their background – the men, the social and historical environment – and try to pick up on the essence of the play, which is the very strong relationships between the women.*

Once we'd made this decision, we had to find a basic level from which to work because the basic level in Chekhov's play (the crucial motivating force) is the soldiers who are billeted in the sisters' home town, and the soldiers were cut in our version. As a basis for our performance, we eventually decided to use the character of Anfisa. In Chekhov's play Anfisa is a small role for an old woman who comes on to the stage from time to time. For us, she would have two roles: she would be a servant, but she would also be a kind of presenter, a creator who builds a theatre in the eyes of the spectators. To enable her to do this we decided to use some lines from Act One of The Seagull. *Anfisa comes on and tells the audience that the play will begin soon. '[W]e must have a theatre', she continues (Chekhov 1967:236). 'Well, this is our theatre'(ibid.: 234). So, when the illusion starts, it's obvious.*

This is also the nature of theatre. Everything is obvious there also. It's always light, technique, actors, etc. But it's also the one place in the world where people come wanting the actors to lie to them. They want to be told that it's 'real time'. Everybody knows that this is untrue, but they all want to believe that it's true. It's extraordinary and wonderful this assumption that the audience will believe that it is, for example, Shakespeare's time. The first level of agreement is already achieved, so we can say, "OK. Now we'll start".

The ritual: *Andrzej's and my preception was that our play would be a kind of ritual that the sisters could constantly repeat in the hope that something might change. My understanding of the women in the original play is that they try to live but can't find a way to do this. When they talk about Moscow, it's an ideal place where everything is fantastically beautiful. This is completely unrealistic, but they continue to dream because only dreams make sense of their lives. They don't understand how to live in the present. They are always waiting for something that will never come.*

The only person who is really in the present is Natasha. She is of course cruel and we are not meant to like her, but she is the one realistic person in the play. She knows what her aim in life is, and she focuses on this very concretely, but the sisters make nothing of their lives. They remain at the same point, dreaming about

Moscow, accepting what happens to them without liking it. Irena says repeatedly that she must work, but later she tries many jobs and hates them all. She's disappointed because of the discrepancy between dream and reality. It is this discrepancy that is I think the point for structuring the characters in this play. The mistake the sisters make is that they try to find a solution, but they don't try to find any distance from themselves. They love and hate each other, but they are stuck in their situation because they never find a perspective from which to view it. This is why, once the sisters come on to the grey square that is our central playing area, they don't leave it until the end of the performance. It's a kind of trap that they don't know they're in.

Natasha and Anfisa come in and out. Anfisa loves the sisters. She's very emotional with them. She tries to help them because she knows that she's the person who must enable them to repeat the ritual – so that they have a chance of discovering an inner solution – but often she sees them become more set, more tragic, as they are lost in the memories they are repeating, and then she starts to cut to a different bit of the play.

Finding a visual aesthetic: I don't see any sense in repeating what's already in the words. I think that each performance should create a world just for that performance, for the time the characters exist on the stage. It shouldn't compare itself with life or with any other performance. It should just be its own world. We've tried to create a very special aesthetic with everything working together on the same level of performance – actors, design, lights, music, text.

In theatre nothing is really new. There is only how to use the elements, how to connect them, to build a structure. As well as adapting the text, Andrzej prepared the design project. Our script has twenty-three scenes, plus a prologue and an epilogue, and we have a window and three chairs on stage all the time. The window is the most important feature. It means something individual for each of the sisters, and it is the place where they can really speak aloud what they are thinking and feeling. From an early stage Andrzej knew the points at which the window would be important, and also its position on stage.

Visually, we wanted the performance to be sparse and rather cold. The colours are monochromatic. The square on the floor is grey. Natasha wears a whitey-grey dress. Irena is in whitey-grey and grey. Masha wears grey, Olga dark grey and black, and Anfisa is in black. It is partly to emphasise the idea that 'this is [a] theatre'. This is our basic colour. Also, we wanted to give the impression of black and white photographs. Several times in rehearsal I used the example of the performance being like a family picture, but a picture from which some of the people have been cut away.

The photographic element of *Three Sisters*

In Chekhov's *Three Sisters* Second Lieutenant Fedotik on two occasions takes photographs of his fellow characters, asking them first to 'Wait half a minute'

(*Chekhov* 1959: 270), or to 'Wait a moment' (ibid: 311); to make, in other words, a temporary suspension in their lives. These suspended moments can be seen as a kind of visual signature for the whole play, because, in *Three Sisters*, the action at points appears to momentarily freeze, to hang suspended, with the result that an audience member, or a reader, retains images of photographs in a mental album once a performance or reading of the text is over. One such photograph, for example, might depict Masha taking off her hat near the beginning of Act One, having decided, after meeting Vershinin and hearing him talk, that she will stay to lunch after all. Another might capture Natasha's predatory passage through a dimly-lit room, candle in hand, and looking, as Chekhov wrote in a letter to Stanislavski, like Lady Macbeth (quoted in Styan 1971: 208, n. 1). Successive images from Acts Three and Four would show a sequence of time frames of events, first in Olga's and Irena's bedroom on the night of the fire, and then in the Prozorovs' garden, while, offstage, the regiment prepares for departure. In the final photograph the sisters would be huddled together as they strain to hear the last, faint notes of the military band that is accompanying the soldiers on their way. Around them would be placed other figures: Chebutykin reading his newspaper, Andrey pushing a pram, Koolyghin smiling in happy relief now that Vershinin, his wife's lover, has left with the regiment.

The photographic quality of *Three Sisters* is already evident in its initial moments. The play begins with the three young women, each immersed in her own individual world. Olga, in the 'regulation dark-blue dress of a secondary school mistress' is ostensibly correcting her pupils' work, but is actually caught up in a web of memories. 'Masha, in a black dress, is sitting reading a book . . . Irena, in white, stands lost in thought' (ibid: 249). The window is open, and, outside, the sun is shining. It is the fifth of May, Irena's Saint's day, a few seconds before midday. Further photographs (defined or suggested by the text), a few moments later, reveal slight changes in their positions. In one, Masha has pursed her lips as she whistles, while Olga perhaps lifts her hand towards her head which, she complains, is aching; in another, Irena's face is turned joyfully towards the lovely weather outside the window. Olga's opening speech furthers the photographic element of the play through its evocation of visually powerful memories: the sisters' father's death 'exactly a year ago' (ibid.), his funeral, and moments in the shared narrative of the sisters' earlier lives in Moscow. Irena initially interrupts this reverie with advice to forget the past and to focus on the loveliness of the present, but then reinforces Olga's memories of Moscow with others of her own. Shortly after the play begins, three new characters, Chebutykin, Toozenbach and Soliony enter the stage picture – the photograph – from an upstage entrance, and their presence and dialogue serve both to complement and comment on the downstage women.

In their production of *The Sisters*, Katarzyna Deszcz, Andrzej Sadowski and the Scarlet Theatre actors utilised the photographic quality of Chekhov's play, both visually and thematically. The tightly controlled groupings of the characters, and the minimalised gestures were choreographed to be seen from the front. The colours of the set, and of the costumes (variations of grey apart from Anfisa's black) were muted as in old photographs. When the characters came to life, and stepped out of the photograph album, it was to act out memories. In *Three Sisters* Olga's opening speech establishes the sisters' investment in the past. In the Scarlet production the past had mostly blotted out the present. Stuck within grooves of individual, and increasingly, too, of shared, remembrances, the sisters reactivated the defining moments in their lives, before the regiment vanished from their home town. When they seemed about to sink hopelessly into wells of personal pain and loss, Anfisa moved between them, prompting them to return to the task in hand — the ritual.

And there was also Natasha, who, in the words of the company's publicity handout, crept in 'through the back door' of the sisters' home, and swept 'through their world ... rearranging the furniture and snuffing out candles'.

The Sisters in performance

Prologue

'The play will be on soon. But we must have a theatre. Well, this is our theatre.'
(Andrzej Sadowski's adaptation based on Chekhov 1967: 233-6)

A grey square on the stage floor – a minimalist representation of the confines of a room – a large, free-standing French window upstage centre, four dangling overhead lights, unlit as yet, in large cone-shaped shades, an audience chatting quietly. Music begins: superficially jaunty, but with a grinding and relentless undertone. Enter stage right a thin, angular, black-clad figure. Her face is pale, her hair scraped severely back into a bun. One long arm is stretched out in front of her, index finger pointing straight ahead.

Using tiny rapid steps, she glides across the stage, turning to look conspiratorially at the audience as she does so. Briefly, she disappears, then re-enters stage left carrying a straight-backed chair which she positions carefully on the grey square. It is the start of the performance – or, at least, the prologue to the main action. It 'will be on soon', the woman, Anfisa promises (Chekhov 1967: 233). First, however, a theatre is needed, and that is what she is constructing. Soon the characters will enter: her outstretched arms indicate where each one will be, and the dimensions of the space within which the awaited act of theatre will take place. Then, on the stage she has created, she speaks words that were originally uttered on another improvised (Chekhovian) stage, Nina's lines from Act One of *The Seagull*: 'Men, lions, eagles .... denizens of the deep .... creatures invisible – that is, all life, has completed its melancholy cycle and died' (ibid.: 240).

The lights fade and, when they come up again, the three sisters are in place on the grey stage. Olga sits downstage right, studying her hands, caught in a circle of illumination from one of the lights overhead. Behind her, Masha is standing in shadow. Irena is just left of centre, lit, like Olga, by an overhead light. Her hands decorously in front of her, she stands, still and stiff in her pale, moth-coloured costume as a clockwork doll whose mechanism has run down. These are the beings who have 'completed [their] melancholy cycle and died', but Anfisa has called them back to re-enact the past within the present moment of theatre.

The Ritual: Part One (scenes 1–15)

1. 'It's exactly a year ago today since Father died'

The ritual begins in silence. Each sister stands or sits motionlessly, imprisoned in the surrounding darkness, marooned in a private limbo-land where even memory is distant and hard to focus on. Then, slowly, with lengthy pauses, Olga begins her first speech, staring all the time at her hands, as though the images she is describing – her father's funeral and the early happy days in Moscow – are gradually becoming imprinted there.

The first line, 'It's exactly a year ago today since Father died' (Chekhov 1964: 73), is followed by a silence as if Olga has forgotten what comes next. Then Irena laughs, loudly and abruptly, a sudden explosive burst of energy which is then succeeded by a return to her former stillness. As Olga proceeds with her speech, she is interrupted occasionally by further spasms of laughter from Irena, and sometimes also by a strange little stumbling movement as though Irena begins to fall and the movement is then arrested. Masha paces to and fro, moving in and out of shadow. From time to time she whistles. Gradually a very faint connection begins to establish itself between Olga and Irena (the two most clearly illuminated figures), which is activated by the word 'Moscow'. Though they never look at, or acknowledge each other in any way, their voices become more vibrant and Irena's face grows more animated. Masha takes no apparent notice of either of them, but she begins to recite the words from Pushkin's 'Ruslan and Lyudmila' which are her equivalent of Moscow: 'A green oak by a curving shore, / And on that oak a chain of gold' (ibid.: 77). This is a mantra that, if she could only understand its significance, would give a validating pattern of meaning to her life, but the words are hollow and empty for her. Despairing of finding any connection with their inner meaning, she suddenly announces her determination to go home, to leave Irena's Saint's-

The Sisters, Scarlet Theatre Company, 1995. Performers: Gráinne Byrne as Olga, with Emma Bernard as Irena in the background. Photo: Sean Mooney

day celebration, and, effectively, also, the ritual. Olga is surprised at first, but then tells Masha that she understands. It seems that, perhaps, she too will refuse to relive the events of the fifth of May. The recently activated ritual appears to be about to break down. Waxworks from a former era into whom faint stirrings of life have been breathed, the sisters will return to their former immobility.

2. A cake from Protopopov

The danger is averted by Anfisa who twice rushes on stage, first with a cake (a present from Protopopov) and then with a samovar. Effectively, Anfisa is a director who presents the sisters with a Stanislavskian exercise. The cake and the samovar are physicalised given circumstances which, together, provide the sisters with the means of entering into an emotion memory.

Once she has refocused them on their shared past of Irena's Saint's day, Anfisa nudges them back to the script of the ritual. They should have started lunch long ago, she tells them. Olga and Irena return to their speculations about Moscow and Masha decides to stay for lunch after all. The stage is set for the fifth character to appear.

3. Enter Natasha

In Chekhov's play Natasha, the 'Petty, little bourgeois housewife' (Chekhov 1959: 289), as Masha terms her, is vulgar and predatory. Obsessed with trivia, she is nevertheless – or perhaps for this very reason – clear-sighted about what she wants and how to get it. In *The Sisters* she is, at one and the same time, a super-realist and a grotesque. Monstrous, yet banal, her aim is to take over the house bit by bit while the sisters remain lost in their dreams of Moscow. From her first entrance her intentions are evident in her body posture. Shoulders raised self-deprecatingly to her ears, head thrust arrogantly forward, her body expresses in embryo the progression she will make from patronised outsider to mistress of the house. In order to find the necessary tone of voice to enable her to get what she wants, she speaks each line twice, trying out its effect. Unlike the sisters, Natasha has no need of Stanislavskian exercises to grasp two important things about theatre: it takes place in the present moment and it is concerned with objectives. She pays no heed to the sisters' possible objectives, only to her own, but this gives her a disturbing strength. While the sisters mentally traverse realms of memory and longing, not knowing why they are doing so, Natasha concentrates on the immediate and realisable. When Masha begins once again to speak the lines about the oak and the curving shore (her version of the Moscow leit motiv), with their yearning for another place and time, Natasha grabs hold of the situation. **This** is theatre, **here** and **now**. Well,

The Sisters, Scarlet Theatre Company, 1995. Performer: Linda Kerr Scott.
Photo: Sean Mooney.

she will use it to conjure up her own desired present moment: the beginning of Act Two of Chekhov's play when, candle in hand, a bourgeois Lady Macbeth, she is already beginning to assert her control over the house.

4. Here and now

Natasha's first words of this, her Act-Two, self are spoken in a consciously deeper, more commanding voice than the one she has used previously. 'It's carnival week', she announces, 'and the servants are in such a state anything might happen – you need eyes in the back of your head' (Chekhov 1964: 92). Previously a gauche and unconfident visitor to the house, she is now free to prowl through the rooms and corridors at will. She has already begun to assert her authority over the servants. Her next move will be to demonstrate the same control over the sisters. Her little son, Bobik, would be happier in a warmer room – Irena's for instance. After all, now that Irena has started to work at the post office, she only uses her room to sleep in. She is never at home during the day, so she can easily move in with Olga.

5. Masha's window scene

Through Anfisa's utilization of Stanislavskian exercises, and Natasha's forcible bringing of the past into the present the sisters are afforded the oportunity of entering into a fuller communication with their own pasts. Memories which have until now been fitfully glimpsed only on the edges of their mental vision begin to assume the lineaments of the here and now.

Masha is the first of the sisters to avail herself of this opportunity, and, as will be the case for Olga and Irena, the intensity of her communication with the past within the present is expressed through her relationship with the window. Standing behind the window, which is upstage centre, she reaches out towards it, as though the past (now become the present) is reflected on its smooth surface. 'What a noise the stove's making', she says (ibid.: 96), and the words evoke for her the moment in Act Two when Vershinin declared his love for her. Her body pressed against the length of the window pane, she becomes first Vershinin telling her of his love and then herself answering him, at one moment telling him to stop and then cancelling out this command: 'No, it's all right, go on, I don't care' (ibid.). Throughout her speech her mouth is pressed hard to the window so that the pane mists up and her face blurs like that of a figure in a dream. Music accompanies her words: pretty, tinkling, musical-box sounds, but cold too and sharp, like ice tears.

6. Holding on to the dream of Moscow – tea, patience, chocolates

In Act One of *Three Sisters* Irena speaks joyfully of the purposefulness of work. She is young, intelligent, healthy. She will get a job, put all her energies into it, and this will give meaning to her life until she is able to go to Moscow. By Act Two however she is already finding her job at the post office tedious and unfulfilling. She must look for another job, she determines, and in the meantime she will dream of Moscow.

Scene Six of *The Sisters* begins with Irena falling stiffly to the ground, an action which completes her earlier, arrested, stumbling movement, revealing it to be the outcome of tiredness and despondency. Her periodic outbursts of forced, over-loud laughter also gain a context because, when she gets to her feet, she speaks of her dream of Moscow, but then follows this with an abrupt staccato laugh which acts as an ironic comment on her words. Then, loudly and insistently, as though to drown out any counter statement that might query the possible fulfilment of her hopes, she begins to count off the months that must pass before June when she and Olga plan to move to Moscow, the place they depend on to give their lives meaning. Caught up in the urgency of Irena's feelings, Masha executes one of her characteristic stamps and swift energetic turns, but this is succeeded by a sense of purposelessness: depressed by winter, yet unable to imagine summer, she exists in a limbo-like waste land that is dreary, dark and featureless.

Masha's mood suggests a possible return to her immobility at the beginning of Scene One. The ritual is once again in danger of grinding to a halt, and Anfisa intervenes swiftly, rushing on with the trolley, this time bearing tea. The ritual continues. Irena describes the likely outcome of the game of patience she is mentally engaged in. Surely it is a good omen that the game is 'going to come out' (ibid.: 97). They will go to Moscow after all. Masha enters more deeply into the Act-Two scenario of *Three Sisters* that is the script for this stage of the ritual. 'I say, what happened to the chocolates?' she asks (ibid.: 102), using words that, in the original text, are Toozenbach's, not her own. In *Three Sisters* Irena provides the explanation (Soliony ate them), but here there is no explanation. The words are an echo of partly-remembered, but scarcely understood events. Like the Pushkin quotation, they are, for Masha, a puzzle she cannot unravel.

7. Fragments, noise, confusion

As though Masha's speculation on the whereabouts of the chocolates in a house that she already thinks of as her property has called her into being, Natasha, the all-seeing eye, now speedily enters from stage right. She stops, adjusts her body image so that it becomes more commanding, exits, and then immediately re-enters stage left. Irena retreats behind the window, and Masha shouts that she wants to be left in peace. Olga complains of her aching head. Anfisa, the presenter/director moves swiftly around the edges of the square, her pointing finger guiding the audience to significant words and actions. This is how it was, this is how it is.

8, 9 and 10. Irena's first window sequence

Positioned, like Masha in scene five, behind the window, and accompanied by similarly sweet, plaintive, yet glassy music, Irena begins **her** first communication with the window (which she has pushed to centre stage), not pressed voluptuously against it as Masha was, but staring up at it like a small child. Her reverie is interrupted by Natasha who raps sharply on the window in Irena's face, following this with a 'request' that Irena should share Olga's bedroom, leaving hers free for Natasha's son, Bobik. Bewildered by what is happening, Irena pushes the window to downstage centre and then, when Natasha has exited, speaks to it softly and despairingly words which in Chekhov's play are motivated by her inability to return Baron Toozenbach's love, and by Soliony's unwelcome attentions: 'Don't ask questions, I'm tired' (ibid.: 108). This is followed by her reiteration of the word 'Moscow', until, like a a gramophone record on which the needle has stuck, she stutters to a halt. 'So many words', she says. 'No words' (*The Sisters*, Sadowski's adaptation: 8).

11. Olga's window scene

On her realization that the dream of Moscow is fading, Irena has pushed the window in front of Olga who, during all the preceding action, has been minutely studying her hands. Confronted by the window, Olga moves, as did her sisters, into the most private and vulnerable realm of memory. For Olga, however, there is no lover, only weariness and an inability to imagine change.

12. 'Don't send me away, Miss Olga' – the shouting match

Realising that Olga is becoming too deeply involved within tragic memories, Anfisa (the director figure) rushes on to the grey square and takes control of the window, at the same time speaking lines from her Act-Three *Three Sisters*'persona as the old nurse, 'Don't send me away, Miss Olga' (Chekhov 1964: 111). Speedily moving the window to centre stage, she spins it round wildly. Her words and actions are effective in that Olga forgets her unhappiness and, getting to her feet for the first time, offers her chair to Anfisa, who, she realises, is tired. Natasha enters, takes in what is going on, spits with great deliberation, and then screams at the old woman for being seated when she – Natasha – is in the room. Alive now (at least temporarily) to what is happening around her, Olga berates Natasha for her treatment of Anfisa, and a shouting match ensues between herself and Natasha. Positioned one each side of the trolley, which is centre stage, they alternately yell at each other, each of them leaning over her opponent as she does so, and causing her to bend backwards. The bout ends with the two of them

The Sisters, Scarlet Theatre Company, 1995. Performers: Gráinne Byrne as Olga (left) and Jan Pearson as Natasha. Photo: Sean Mooney

upright, faces close together. Natasha has the last word: Olga must move to another part of the house, or they will be forever quarrelling.

13. An interjection from *The Seagull*

Scene Thirteen consists of a one-line interjection from *The Seagull*, 'It's an odd play, isn't it?' (Chekhov 1967: 244), a metatheatrical reminder to the audience of the nature of the event they are watching and an ironic comment on the previous scene.

14. 'No words'

As she did in Scene Ten, Irena repeats 'Moscow' over and over again in a fierce, driving rhythm, and then sadly and plaintively, 'So many words, no words'. The jumble of thoughts in her head has focused on just one word, 'Moscow', but now this too is becoming faint and indecipherable.

15. The ritual breaks down

Standing between her two sisters, so that the three of them form a line upstage centre facing the audience, Masha gives vocal form to **her** jumble of thoughts and longings that, like Irena's, will then fade away into silence. Two questions stand out sharply from the rest of her words: 'Is somebody here? Who is it?' (Sadowski's adaptation: 10) but, as with her query about the chocolates, there is no answer from the surrounding darkness, and Masha returns to her earlier repetition of the Pushkin quotation, which she articulates over and over like Irena's insistent repetition of the word 'Moscow'. After her final 'And on that oak a chain of gold' Masha falls silent, though her lips continue to move. The other characters also soundlessly mouth lines from their earlier sections of dialogue. Then the driving rhythms of the prologue music are heard again.

A Recapitulation

A shortened, more jagged version of the prologue is enacted, followed by an edited version of the first three scenes. The sequence ends with Natasha repeatedly congratulating Irena on her Saint's day. Each time she first looks slyly round to see that everyone is watching, then kisses Irena on the cheek. Irena responds to each kiss with mechanical-sounding laughter. The third time she laughs she falls heavily to the floor protesting that she has had as much as she can take. She then, however, gets up, and takes control of the ritual, restarting it at the point it had come to a halt, but moving it also into a new, more intense phase.

The Sisters, Scarlet Theatre Company, 1995. Performers: (left to right) Gráinne Byrne as Olga, Helen Anderson as Masha and Emma Bernard as Irena. Photo: Sean Mooney

The Ritual, Part Two (scenes 16-23)

16. Lights, window, confusion

In the first part of the ritual each sister has established her individual physical rhythm. Olga's is slow, controlled, with occasional outpourings of pain or anger. Masha's is proud, upright. She is a tightly-wound coil that threatens to spring into quivering life, yet never quite does so. Irena performs odd truncated movements and vocalizations: a stumble that only once proceeds to a fall, a quickly erased ghost of a smile, a disproportionately loud bark of laughter that leaves no trace behind. For each of them there has been a sequence with the window which has revealed something deeper, more lyrical, haunting, tragic.

When Irena restarts the ritual (after the brief, recapitulatory, opening section), moving still deeper into the core of memory, she utilises, not the window, but, instead, other atmospheric stage objects: the overhead lights. Crying out in despair, because the radiant and purposeful life in which she has believed is slipping away from her, and it seems that she will never now go to Moscow, she repeatedly swings the lights so that they rock wildly from side to side. Olga, Masha and Natasha respond with characteristic gestures. Natasha grabs hold of the swinging light above her, holding on to what she views as her property. Masha stamps and turns, arrogantly and ecstatically beneath her plunging light, and Olga moves to and fro beneath hers holding her hands upwards, bathing them in the soft warmth. As Irena's fit of despair slows, then halts, Olga continues to perform a little side-to-side dance step, her illuminated hands stretched in front of her, palms upwards so that it seems as if she reads there the script of the advice she proceeds to give Irena: 'marry the baron. After all you do respect him' (ibid.: 120).

By way of response, Irena pushes the window to a diagonal centre-stage position and stands behind it so that she is facing towards Olga who is downstage right. She then opens the window, for the first time, and speaks through the aperture. She has been waiting for so long, she tells Olga, to go to Moscow, thinking that there she would meet a man she could genuinely love, but it has all turned out to be nonsense. This giving voice to her grieving sense of loss is followed, and counterpointed, by Masha's ringing declaration of her love for Vershinin, love that she has previously only confided to the window. Now Masha stands proudly upstage left, and speaks in the direction of the opened window, and towards Olga, who, determined not to listen, closes the window and crosses downstage left. Irena's response is to open the window again and turn it to face Olga, thus forcing her to listen to Masha, who has crossed to upstage right, with the result that the sisters are again positioned in a diagonal line. Masha continues with her confession, and, in a renewed attempt to stop her, Olga once more closes the window. Irena determinedly reopens it, and, stepping through it, Masha goes up close to Olga and completes her story of her love for Vershinin.

17. 'Nowhere like Moscow'

First pushing the open window back to centre stage, Irena then replicates Masha's action by stepping through it. For Irena, to whom the window has been a mirror-world where she has talked, like a child, to imaginary figures (sometimes a replica of herself, sometimes a lover), her movement through the open window signifies her crossing into a new dimension. Like Lewis Carroll's Alice, she enters a looking-glass world, but only to find that it closely resembles the place she has left. The first thing that awaits her is a sound, a perturbing knocking. Where from? What is it? An everyday noise capable of rational explanation? A warning of approaching disaster? A measuring of time? Whatever it is, and means, its beat follows the metronomic pulsing of her own dark anxieties, and, in a last attempt to escape them, she determines to pay the necessary price and so to find a way into light, and space, and freedom. She will marry the baron if only they can 'go to Moscow …. There's nowhere in the world like Moscow' (ibid.: 123).

18. The window as evidence of power

All the objects used in the production are essentially functional. Before the performance began they were drab and ordinary. It is only through the act of theatre that the lights and window, transformed by a Stanislavskian 'magic if', have become something more than their pre-show mundane selves. Unlike the sisters, Natasha has never used the window as a magic object. The first of the characters (apart from Anfisa as presenter) to conjure up the here and now of theatre, she did so for strictly limited and utilitarian motives. First she rehearsed her planned take-over bid of the sisters' house, then, having mastered the necessary moves and tonal inflexions, she acted. The present moment of theatre she brought into being was in no way extraordinary to her. It was a trick, something to be used as a means of gaining control.

Now, she demonstrates the degree of control she has achieved, using the window, which is positioned centre stage and facing the audience, to do so. The area upstage of the window at this point represents the outside of the house, and here the sisters can be seen, huddled together, looking into the place from which Natasha has exiled them. To emphasise her authority, Natasha twice orders Anfisa to get out of the room and then to come in again. Anfisa exits through the window, re-enters, exits, re-enters, opening and closing the window each time.

The Sisters, Scarlet Theatre Company, 1995. Performers: (left to right) Gráinne Byrne as Olga, Emma Bernard as Irena and Helen Anderson as Masha. Photo: Sheila Burnett.

19. The window as burden

Anfisa spins the window round and the sisters move into the downstage area which, in its turn, becomes representative of the outside of the house. Olga and Masha stand motionlessly stage right, their upper bodies softly lit from above, their lower bodies draped in darkness. Irena stands centre, holding on to the window, which is behind her, and affirms the decisions she has now made: to give up all hope of Moscow, to marry the baron and to devote herself to work. But something has happened the previous night outside the local theatre, some incident no-one will tell her about, but which she fears will somehow have a disastrous effect on her life. She interrupts her speech occasionally with sudden bursts of laughter, or by pushing hard against the window, which she continues to hold on to all the time as if it is a burden that she is unable to relinquish. At the end of her speech she turns to the window and knocks on it, seeking helplessly to be let in, to somehow understand what has happened.

20 and 21. Further questions, darkness, an answer?

At first, Irena continues intermittently to knock at the window, while, upstage right, Masha paces in a circular, self-perpetuating motion, her thoughts focused on her lover, Vershinin, who is about to leave the town with his regiment. Irena then stops knocking on the window, and speaks instead to an imagined Toozenbach, enquiring where he is going, and what the true facts are about yesterday's incident. Olga imagines the next day when the town will be empty of soldiers. The sisters will remain here with their memories. They will never go to Moscow.

Then, loudly and urgently, Masha returns to her repetition of the Pushkin quotation, the noise of her feet as they pace to and fro keeping time with the words. The second time she speaks the words 'a chain of gold' the overhead lights go out leaving the stage virtually in darkness. In a partial evocation of the earlier sequence when Irena pushed the lights to and fro, Olga, Irena and, this time, Anfisa run from one light to another, though now there is no illumination, and they stare up into the gloom. Masha continues to pace and to call out the words of the quotation. Like Irena earlier, she finds that the words mix themselves up in her mind. There is no shape, no pattern, apart from the 'curving shore', but what does that mean? Why does its image pound endlessly in her head?

There is a momentary silence, followed by a brief return to the previous confusion, then stillness and deeper darkness. When the lights come up again, Masha is revealed sitting on a chair upstage centre. Each side of her is an empty chair, and the positioning of the three chairs, facing the audience, echoes the straight-line formation in which the sisters stood at the end of the first part of the ritual. Natasha is standing to their right, and she begins to detail her plans now that she has fully taken control of the house. She will move her husband into the room that Irena has been sleeping in, and put her little girl in his room. In addition, she intends to cut down the old avenue of fir trees in the garden and plant flowers in their place. There is no hesitation in her speech now, no repetition or trying out of new inflexions. Natasha has found the voice and gestures she has been searching for. She is strident, vulgar, a caricature of a successful middle-class wife and mother, but she is powerful. Nevertheless, Irena apparently finds her funny. She begins to laugh, almost choking in her attempt to keep the fact hidden. Faintly, Olga joins in, making little smothered gusts of sound. Masha smiles. However covertly, they are mocking Natasha and enjoying doing so. Is this perhaps a solution, a way out of the ritual?

22. 'Curtain!'

Yes, the end appears to be in sight. We can go home now, Olga tells her sisters. Anfisa rushes on, and standing with her arms raised, a director stopping the show, she quotes again from *The Seagull*: 'The play.. [i]s over. Enough! Curtain!' (Chekhov 1967: 242), and Olga takes up the refrain, 'Enough ... enough ... enough'. She and Masha begin to move away.

23. Stasis

The play within the play of *The Seagull* ends only because Konstantin, its author and director, suspends its action. It has not reached its conclusion. Anfisa has followed Konstantin's example and stopped her play, in her case because the ritual she has created has seemingly reached a point where its purpose has been achieved.

Her intention is defeated by Irena who remains seated and continues to laugh, whether happily or hysterically it is difficult to say. Olga and Masha return, and Olga tells Irena that the baron has been killed in a duel. They are now moving towards the ultimate moments of *Three Sisters*, which have been brought into being so that the sisters may have a chance to rewrite them. The 'now' of stage time and of the ritual is fusing with the 'now' of the final photographic images of *Three Sisters*. Irena makes a slow, dreadful, retching sound, the source (finally revealed) of her weird dissociated laughter, which she then swallows, gulps down, erases. She sits facing front, while, behind her, Masha places consoling hands on her shoulders. Olga sits, turned away. As at the conclusion of the first phase of the ritual, they speak together, though, in contrast to that earlier point, what they are saying can now be heard. From the jumble of sounds, certain strings of words emerge: 'listen to the band ... what is all this for? ... left alone ... work ... We still have our lives ... autumn ... winter' (Chekhov 1964: 138&9), and, in addition, but very softly, Olga's description of the music of the band, 'cheerful, happy' (ibid.: 139). It is the one bright note. Quickly, the sisters get to their feet and exit.

Epilogue

Kneeling centre stage, Anfisa speaks Nina's lines from Konstantin's play in *The Seagull* which she spoke at the beginning of the performance, though, then, she was the creator utilising them to facilitate the event she was trying to call into being. Whereas, before, her utterance of Nina's words was loud and incantatory, it is now quiet and wondering: 'all life - has completed its melancholy cycle and died'. Death and melancholy seek to obliterate evidence of the strangeness and beauty of life, but do not quite succeed. The grinding rhythms of the prologue music are heard. Alert now, Anfisa gets to her feet and assumes again the sharply angular and linear movements of her presenter persona. Following her outstretched arm and pointing finger, she exits stage right – to the place, in other words, from which she originally came. The ritual has got as far as it can, this time, but tomorrow it can be replayed, and maybe then it will get further.

Comments on the rehearsal process by the director and the actors

Katarzyna Deszcz – *finding a theatre language*: *For each of the characters I wanted to find a special theatre language because I didn't want to create simply a psychological women's play. Of course the psychological relationships are there at a fundamental level, but I wanted to find a way of showing something other than that. The basis from which we started rehearsals was the search for a rhythm for each character. We began with very rhythmical exercises. For the first hour I asked the cast to explore individual rhythms, just through walking, and, at the same time, to read the text aloud without stopping and without gestures. Later, they continued with the walking exercise, but without their texts. They could use their voices but not in a verbal sense, and they had to keep the same situations and rhythms. Starting from this early work, they gradually developed their own characteristic organic rhythms which they use now in performance.*

The sisters all have points when it seems that they won't be able to continue with the ritual, and then there is a break in their rhythms. In order to clarify this I made a diagram showing the twenty-three scenes, plus the prologue and the epilogue, and noting where something important, like a break of rhythm, happens for each character. I also noted down the position of the window in each scene, and of the trolley Anfisa brings on when this is on stage. I find this rather mathematical way of working very helpful. It helps to remind me of the structure, how all the scenes work together. It's a kind of auto-control system. From time to time I come back to it, and say, "Oh, my God! It must be this timing!" Otherwise there's a risk that I'll get lost in the work. Of course one also has to be open to what the actors are doing.

Despite all my and Andrzej's preparations there are lots of things I really don't know when I start work on a new performance, and it's fascinating this sense of never being absolutely ready. I will know, for example, what the structure of the performance is, and its subject matter, what I want the characters to use, and what I must do at a particular time, but the most exciting element is the adventure with the actors, the fact that you don't, absolutely, know what you're doing. I love this about the work, that it's never the same.

Working with British actors: *One excellent thing about working with British actors is that they have very good discipline in the work. This is extremely helpful. In Poland it's typical for actors to want to discuss things at length at the beginning of rehearsals because they have different ideas from those of the director. Of course sometimes these ideas are helpful, but it's a question of proportion. The director's ideas may not be any good, but the essential thing is to check them out on the stage. Then, if they don't work, we can search for something else, rather than sit around a table for two weeks endlessly discussing. The professional attitude of British actors comes I think partly from the fact that so many actors here are unemployed. They're desperate to do something. Polish actors have a much better situation. More of them are employed.*

The difficult thing about working with British actors is that they have a very great respect for the words. I realise that this is a generalisation, but in British theatre it seems to me that the main point is to present the text. Everything else is secondary. With Polish actors this isn't really a problem. For many years they've been used to using the text as a pretext to say something else. So, there is this big difference. Here, the words mean what they mean, and it's sometimes very difficult to say to an actor, "It's done, so you don't need to show it. Try to find something new, to build something between the text you are speaking and this moment, the place where you are, the life that you have." This is the theatre. The theatre is not just to present the text. This I sometimes find difficult.

In fact, though, when the work is going well, there isn't too much difference. Everywhere there are people who love the theatre, and the problems are similar. In the beginning there's the research, and then later the work begins to go well. About ten days before the previews, there is crisis. Nobody likes the production, nothing is working, the director is a completely senseless person. Two or three days before the previews is the major hysterical point. Everyone hates everyone else. And then it's the opening night, and it's going, so that's that.

My work with Scarlet Theatre has been very valuable. I've got a lot of experience from it which I can build on when I return to Poland. So it's not simply a Polish director sharing her work with British actors. It's also the opposite. The co-operation is not just from one side. I like working here. Generally I very much enjoy working with British actors.

Gráinne Byrne (Olga): *I first read Andrzej's adaptation of the play on the ferry going over to Ireland, where we were going to have an initial rehearsal period, and I was completely baffled. It didn't make any sense to me. Then, for a long time in rehearsals, I had no idea how to play Olga. Kasia was very keen that we should be true to our own worlds. It wasn't up to us to show irony, she said. We just had to be absolutely truthful to our own individual worlds which inhabited a larger stage. The problem was that I didn't know what my individual world was. After Anfisa's prologue I'm the first person who speaks and I felt a terrible onus, having to open the piece, coming out with the text, 'It's exactly a year ago that Father died'. Kasia kept saying that I was being too psychological. "Take your time, " she said, "Pause, pause". Everything I tried I felt as if I was being too psychological and I didn't know what to do for ages. I felt that it would be my fault if the show wasn't a success because I set the tone.*

The saving factor was that I trusted Kasia completely because I thought that the way she'd dealt with actors in an earlier workshop she'd done with us was so sensitive and spot-on. She was able to identify people's problems - habits that they'd grown into, things which had worked for them once but had now become clichéd - and to give them tailor-made exercises which made an enormous difference to their performing. So, though I was utterly bewildered, I had complete faith that Kasia knew what she was doing. She felt that we were extremely polite in rehearsals. Evidently in Poland actors argue a lot and we didn't. I was the most obedient I've ever been, surprisingly so. I normally do argue a fair bit, but, in this case, I felt that Kasia knew more than I did.

She is anyway someone who has considerable authority, both as a person and as a director, and also we wanted to be true to her vision. The result was that we didn't really talk about the work very much among ourselves, and I think this helped the work process because it strengthened our sense of being in our own individual worlds. It benefited the show because, when we opened, we were simply being true to what we'd been asked to do. And then Kasia said, "Use your intuition. Start to play it more. It's all been laid down. These are the tracks, but you can grow along them." And it's true. That is exactly what happened. At first I found it difficult to sustain the discipline and I felt that my performance was hollow and forced because the fact that we hadn't been working psychologically had meant that it was difficult to create an emotional through-line, but, about five shows into the run, it became genuinely emotional. The way Kasia worked with us was very strange to me. It wasn't personal work, of the kind I'm used to. We were looking at the characters from the outside, and it was as if they were, for instance, musical instruments. Olga was perhaps an oboe, Irena a flute and Masha a violin. Now, I can feel the way in which the individual instruments work together. I can sense my difference, as Olga, from Masha and Irena, and I know that that difference is crucial to the shape of the whole show.

I think the piece as a whole has something of the quality of a Beckett play. The characters are in limbo-land, and, being a Catholic, I know all about that. As in

Beckett, there's a sense of 'What's it all for?'. The characters are searching for something, and maybe this time one of them will say something that will move them on and effect a reincarnation onto the next plane. One of the ways I explained to myself the fact that they always have to replay the ritual from the beginning is that, when I was a small child in Ireland and my grandmother told me stories, she always started right from the beginning and went all the way through with every detail, absolutely solidly. She would even say what the sky was like, and, for example, whether she had the milk in or not, and that there was a sick cow in the stable. It was the same story exactly, and she'd paint it in such a way that time stood still. They were often tragic stories, of the day that someone died for example, and, for the sisters, the story they're replaying is of the most pivotal time in their lives. The regiment is there, and the chance of marriage, and then they're gone.

Though the play was written nearly a hundred years ago I think Olga is a very modern person. I was talking to some women who came to see the show the other day and they were very upset by it. I think it's because we all have an agenda for our lives. We think we'll perhaps be married and have children by a certain age, and then we realise that maybe it's not going to happen. For the sisters the decisive point in their lives was probably their early twenties. It's later for women now, but the years from perhaps twenty-eight to thirty-six, say, are still very significant for how the rest of your life is going to be. For the sisters the regiment was the decisive factor, but today women can still be caught in the discrepancy between expectation and reality. The difficulty is coming to terms with that. That's what the piece says for me.

Helen Anderson (Masha): *My initial feeling when we started rehearsing was that I didn't know the play well enough to begin working on a compacted version of it. I knew that I needed a fuller understanding of the original before I dived in and pulled out the essence. So I read Chekhov's text a lot at home, looking at what really happens in the scenes, what we had taken out, and what was missing.*

One of the things that I found difficult in the early stages was that Masha's story is perhaps the most difficult of the sisters' stories to tell without the men being there, because she is so directly bound up with them. She's married to one man and in love with another, and that's her tragedy. I worried about whether her situation would be clear for the audience. To begin with, we did speak the men's names. I would say, for example, 'I love Vershinin' when I made my confession, but every time we said the names they would jump out as being something very odd. Because the men never come on to the stage, it was a jolt to hear their names, and, in the end, we took them out. That was where the idea came from for the speech I do behind the window: 'I love you, love you, love you' (Chekhov 1964 : 96). In fact, these are Vershinin's words to Masha that I'm speaking and it's as if I'm looking in a mirror. I'm not looking through the window, I'm looking at my reflection in the glass. That was how we got round the problem in that instance of the man not being there.

The other difficulty I had initially was that Kasia knew exactly what she wanted. I'm not used to this because normally I work on plays that haven't been performed before. With new writing you go into rehearsals on the first day and nobody, including the writer, knows exactly what the play is, and you all find out together. Hopefully the director's a couple of paces ahead of you all the way through, but nevertheless everybody is discovering more or less simultaneously. With The Sisters *this wasn't the case at all. Kasia not only knew what she wanted with regard to how the text should be delivered, she also knew how she wanted it to look, the atmosphere, the 'smell' of it. It felt at first as though we were groping around, trying to hit what Kasia wanted, waiting for the moment when she'd go, "Yes, it's all right", and you'd think, "Whew! I've got something!"*

The previous shows I'd done with Scarlet had all been devised and the process had been very playful. It was very odd to be in a situation where you weren't bouncing off your fellow performers. You weren't interacting and creating things together in that sense at all. What you were doing was creating an effect, but you were doing it by holding your own line against someone else's and that was very disquieting for a long time.

I was fascinated though by the abstract way that we began rehearsals. We spent the first few days just exploring different rhythms: walking in step with one another, walking out of step, speeding up, slowing down, synchronising, syncopating, counterpointing. Gradually, we all developed different pattems of movement. Kasia gave me a figure of eight to work with, and at first I moved in a very measured way, concentrating on my feet all the time. The rhythms that Kasia gave us involved a lot of mental control, and it was very difficult at first to have an emotional journey at the same time as keeping to the movements and rhythms. This worried me to begin with, but gradually I found that the body has a very strong and accurate memory, and it doesn't take long for it to do things automatically. When your head is freed up you can start to integrate everything you've been given. In the early stages the absolute precision Kasia demanded – of timing, movement, tone of voice, rhythm, physical gestures – seemed a huge restriction on our instincts as actors, but, gradually, I think we all came to realise that the visual logic and disciplined style of performance were the things that would enable us to deliver our distillation of the emotional high points in the characters' lives.

In performance I've found more and more the benefit of Kasia's way of working. Because she had such a strong control over the production it took us a long time to make it our own, but now I realise that physical discipline does conversely give you an emotional freedom. With Masha, I find very often that my movements (particularly the stamp and turn that I do) are a way of releasing the emotion. The discipline also serves to keep you away from the danger of becoming hysterical. The production is a very emotional piece and it could become a terrible self-indulgent wallow. The discipline gives you limits and guidelines.

I'm relieved though that the performance only lasts an hour because the level of intensity is extraordinary. One effect of Kasia's way of working was that, in rehearsals, you could never just come in and work on a bit of it. If you tweaked something in a scene, that meant you had to re-rehearse the whole show because everything is in very tight proportion with everything else. It's all very fragile and carefully interwoven, and the slightest change would have a knock-on effect right the way through. This was exhausting in rehearsals because it meant that every time something was changed we had to do a run through. Performances are exhausting also because the tension of the piece never lets up for a moment, and we three sisters all the time inhabit a deeply unpleasant world. We're each isolated in our own thoughts and yet also trapped in a place from which we can't escape – and that's what it feels like.

Emma Bernard (Irena): *An important part of Kasia's work method was to give us technical things that we couldn't necessarily relate to, but that have become pegs on which we hang what we do. They act as a structural safety net and guideline. To some extent it felt like a battle in rehearsals, but, as always when you have a constraint, what that does eventually is to open things out and to force you to express something else. I think that the emotion of the piece comes out of the control we established, and this control was important because the characters' situations are to do with feeling controlled and themselves being out of control.*

The outcome of the ritual

Emma: *Of all the sisters, Irena is the one who really believes that they will go to Moscow, probably because she's the youngest and she's been disappointed less than the other two. She really thinks that they'll get out, and, when they don't, she has a sort of breakdown because she's so shocked that that's it. There is no more.*

Helen: *The idea is that the ritual is played out in the hopes that something will change and the outcome will be different. The thing that does change is that Irena effectively says, "No, I can't do this any more. I can't keep going over this." So what happens is that they move on to what occurred next, which normally they're too scared to go over. They begin to relive events that are painful. It's all quite fresh and raw. For Masha, the crucial thing is her confession of her love for Vershinin. Once she's made it, she realises how completely alone she is, and that she will never be understood by her sisters. She's going to have to live the rest of her life with this obsession and regret. Her life is wasted, as she sees it. I think that the closest we ever come to being sisters is at the very end when Olga and I have begun to exit and then we come back to reassure Irena. It's almost the only time that we look at each other. Olga and I are collaborating here, trying to break the spell for Irena.*

Gráinne: *When the three of us say our lines together at the end I feel that I'm making a commentary on the whole show. I'm trying to come to a conclusion, to salvage something. I feel that we're still trapped, but it's as if we're on a loop.*

We've reached the maximum outcome possible, but for tonight. It's always for tonight.

Linda Kerr Scott (Anfisa): *Part of my function as Anfisa is to be a kind of mistress of ceremonies who binds all the segments together From time to time the sisters act out this ritual and Anfisa's job is to observe. She can't change anything, but she does try to push some reality into the spaces in their dreams. In her role as the nurse, Anfisa has her own journey. She goes off to live with Olga in the school house. The sisters' story isn't Anfisa's story. She's not going to Moscow. They might, because, apart from the original play, there's nothing that says they won't get there. We've all got this far for tonight, and we know that it's time to stop. We haven't made it elsewhere, but we've got further than before. And we can do it again. It happens again and again.*

A later comment by Gráinne, at the time of the 1996 revival of the production: The Sisters *is about a profound loneliness (shown physically in the separation of the characters) and about a knowledge of what one needs to do, but an inability to do it. There is an intellectual insight, but also a terrible inertia. The ever-fading hope is represented by the lights suspended above the characters, and their emotions by the choreography, particularly the sudden movements when they're disturbed. Working on the piece again I've been struck afresh by what an excellent production it is, and I feel able to say that because of the way Scarlet works, introducing artists, bringing them together. The eventual magic is what is created through this process. What strikes me most about* **The Sisters** *now is its jigsaw quality, how every layer of theatre craft – each piece – fits together absolutely.*

Performance Venues

1995

17 & 18 February	Old Bull Arts Centre	Barnet
22 February	21 South Street	Reading
24 February	Hearth Polish Club	Kensington
25 February	Arts Centre	Colchester
28 February-18 March	Young Vic Studio	London
21 March	Dartington College of Arts	Nr. Totnes
27&28 March	Exeter and Devon Arts Centre	Exeter
30 March	Guidhall Arts Centre	Grantham
1 & 2 April	Jackson's Lane	London
4 April	Queen's Hall	Hexham
5 April	The Hawth	Crawley
7 April	Borough Theatre	Abergavenny
11 April	Old Town Hall	Hemel Hempstead
12 April	Arts Centre	Harrow
14&15 April	Yvonne Arnaud Theatre	Guildford

1996

28 May-1 June	Watermans	Brentford
6&7 June	Slovacki Theatre	Krakow (Poland)
9 June	Teatr Maly	Warsaw (Poland)
10 June 1995	Teatr im Wegierki	Bialystok (Poland)
11&12 June	Teatri Polski	Bydgoszcz (Poland)
13 June	Palac Kultury	Poznana (Poland)
17 June	The Studio	Westminster
12-31 August	Theatre Workshop	Edinburgh
17-19 October	Purcell Room South Bank Centre	London

Press Quotes

'If the rest of the studio's season of experimental theatre is this good, the Young Vic is on to a winner.' (Kate Bassett, *The Times*, 6 March 1995)

'Katarzyna Deszcz's visionary direction [and] Andrzej Sadowski's pointillist script .... succeed in laying bare the essential spirit of *Three Sisters* .... The acting of all five performers is superlative ... *The Sisters* is seriously beautiful.' (Sara Abdullah, *What's On*, 8-15 March 1995)

'a mad, sad dance of desolation, peppered with wit and staged with economical beauty and invention' (Brian Logan, *The Guardian*, 20 August 1996)

'a perfect gem of a production' (Stella Goomey, *The Stage*, 22 August 1996)

Paper Walls, Scarlet Theatre Company. Performers: Joyce Henderson as the Older Daughter, with Christine Entwisle as the Younger Daughter on her shoulders. Photo: Sheila Burnett

Paper Walls

Credits

Director/Designer	Alice Power
Director/Designer	Alice Purcell
Text (in collaboration with the original cast)	Cindy Oswin
Lighting Design	Danielle Bisson and Jo Joelson (touring adaptation)
Original Music	Nigel Piper
Company Manager/Technician	Lucy Barter
Booking Agent	Leila Jancovich of Bathena-Jancovich
Artistic Director	Gráinne Byrne
Administration	Marie Rémy

Cast Lists

Original Team 1994 Tour

The mother: Jan Pearson
The older daughter: Joyce Henderson
The younger daughter: Christine Entwisle

1995 Revival: Edinburgh Run

The mother: Jan Pearson
The older daughter: Gráinne Byrne
The younger daughter: Christine Entwisle

1995 Revival: National Tour and Dates at BAC in London

The mother: Jane Guernier
The older daughter: Gráinne Byrne
The younger daughter: Nicola Blackwell

1996 Revival: London International Mime Festival dates at the Purcell Room and West Yorkshire Playhouse, Jan. and Feb. 1996

The mother: Jan Pearson
The older daughter: Gráinne Byrne
The younger daughter: Christine Entwisle

Gráinne Byrne talking about *Paper Walls*: *The internal world of the three sisters was very apparent, both through monologues and through visual means.*

There were no monologues in Paper Walls, *but the tortured inner selves of the characters were represented in other ways, particularly through the dolls. It was almost as if they were a part of the women that took action on their behalf. It was as if they were spirits.*

Elements of the performance: an audience, three actresses, one muffled 'male' figure (played by one of the actresses), three large dolls, music, assorted props, a shiny dustbin stage right, a shed centre stage. The latter has a small, four-paned window in the top stage right-hand corner of the side facing directly towards the audience. It also has a small skylight and, in the side facing stage left, a narrow door with a latch.

Paper Walls in performance

Semi-darkness. A 'male' figure enters from upstage left, muffled, so that his face cannot be seen, and wearing black gloves. He goes into the shed closing the door sharply behind him. Music begins, overlaid with amplified and distorted washing-up noises. The sounds are funny, childlike and sinister, all at the same time. Activity begins inside the shed. The blind is pulled up at the window, and the panes are slowly and methodically cleaned. The window opens and a young woman puts her arm through the opening and shakes a yellow duster. She is a child playing 'house' or, given the fact that her largeness at the tiny window distorts perceptions of size, a fairy-tale princess in a high tower – Rapunzel perhaps who will later let down her yellow hair so that a fairy-tale prince can climb up to her. The door and skylight open and two hands, each bearing an identical duster, appear. In a stately and synchronised 'dance' they meticulously clean the edges of the door and skylight. The door and the skylight close.

Again the door opens and a woman comes out of the shed with a large bucket. She collects a trolley from stage left, places the bucket on it and pushes it across the front of the stage, pausing to smile at the audience once she reaches centre stage. She exits upstage right. There is the sound of water being poured into the bucket, and the woman reappears pushing, very carefully, the trolley on which the bucket, now filled with water, is perched precariously. She returns the trolley to its stage-left position, and lifts up the heavy bucket, spilling some of the water. Obviously very distressed, she goes into the shed, and immediately a second woman comes hurrying out, carrying a small jug and saying, 'Right, I'll get that. Not to worry' (*Paper Walls*, unpublished script: 6). She hurries over to stage right. Meanwhile the door of the shed bursts open and the first woman is thrown out, and then dragged back in again by a gloved hand. The door shuts. The second woman re-enters with a jugful of water and goes into the shed. A radio is heard and the sound of a kettle boiling. The window steams up and, on it, a finger writes 'Please HEL... '.(ibid.) A gloved hand appears and erases the words. The radio stops. The young woman is seen again at the window, mouthing something. Then she disappears abruptly.

Throughout all this, the audience have been in the position of eavesdroppers who hear only occasional snatches of conversation, with the result that its subject matter is difficult to identify. They have also been witnesses, but of what? A macabre comedy sketch? A child's doll's-house version of a strange and sinister adult world? As the performance continues the audience have to try to work out the clues, to put the pieces of a solution together in order to create a complete jigsaw. Heads appear briefly at the window, speaking snatches of dialogue, or singing fragments of a song. A woman begins to tell a joke, but stops abruptly as she is apparently dragged out of sight. All three women's faces appear at the window. They sing the opening words of a song and are jerked away. One of them, a different woman from the first, is thrust back. She puts her head out of the window and smiles at the audience. 'This is a house like any other house' she says (ibid.). Her words are presumably meant to be reassuring, but they have the opposite effect. Whatever the shed (the house) is, it is clearly not as other houses are, and what goes on inside it is hardly part of the pattern of ordinary life.

Whereas the tiny window offers the audience only glimpses of parts of women's bodies – heads and arms – along with fragments of – possibly incorrect – information about them, the door enables the whole of the women to be seen. Unfortunately, this physical clarity is not matched by a similarly comprehensible view of their story. The women's names, we gradually learn, are Margaret and, confusingly, Jean One and Jean Two. The information that the house is 'like any other house' is followed by sounds of loud sawing and hammering. While this is going on, each woman comes individually out of the door and 'explains' what is happening inside by demonstrating one of the tools that are being used. 'This is a claw hammer', Jean Two tells the audience. 'You can catch yourself a nasty blow with this' (P.W.: 2). Margaret, in her turn, holds up a handsaw, valuable 'for occasional crosscutting and ripping' (ibid.). Jean One demonstrates a gun, the 'household firearm ... useful in the event of burglars' (P.W.: 3). Margaret re-enters with a giant saw which she shows to the audience in silence. She then goes back into the house, holding the saw stiffly out in front of her.

When the women are seen together outside the house, they act always in unison. Dressed in identical red jackets, for example, and to the sound of martial music, they march across the stage and off into the wings, returning, a few seconds later, each holding a B&Q bag. They then do maintenance work on the outside of the house: oiling hinges, hammering nails, and sanding the wood round the window. As they do this, they each in turn speak identical words: 'I'll be getting on with this then' (P.W.: 4). It is a

Paper Walls, Scarlet Theatre Company, 1995 revival. Performers: (left to right) Nicola Blackwell, Jane Guernier and Gráinne Byrne. Photo: Lietta Granato

routine – comic and yet worrying. When Jean One collapses underneath the window (why is not explained) Margaret continues with her sanding while holding Jean One's hand, which is clutching an oil can in position so that she can carry on with her task. None of the women give any indication that what is happening is in any way bizarre.

Later, they reappear, dressed again in their red jackets, Jean Two and Margaret supporting Jean One (who is carrying a washbag) between them. They are on their way to casualty, Jean Two explains brightly. Unfortunately, Jean One has had an accident. They had 'obtained a large billiard table for inside use', and Jean 'was just about to pot the black when she caught herself a nasty blow to the stomach with the cue rest' (ibid.). Throughout Jean Two's speech Jean One, the victim of the related incident, smiles as if the whole thing is a joke. This is cartoon violence that is being described: blows with no resulting pain or blood.

Interspersed with the comic routines however there are brief peturbing glimpses of what may really be going on inside the house. Margaret appears at the window, examining an egg through a magnifying glass. The egg drops from her fingers and her distraught voice is heard exclaiming, 'You've done it again ... oh Margaret, how do you do it? Because you're useless, that's why' (P.W: 3), her anxiety seeming disproportionate for such a minor accident. When Jean Two and Margaret march back from the hospital, having left Jean One there, they go into the house, but Jean Two is immediately thrown out again. A gloved hand reaches out and gives her a euphonium. She begins to play, but stops when she hears Margaret, inside the house, say, 'Please don't make me ... It can't breathe ... I'm sorry ... I am holding it still' (P.W.: 7). The door opens, signalling that Jean Two should begin playing again. From time to time there are sounds of a struggle from inside the house, to which Jean Two responds by stopping playing, but, each time she does so, the door opens forcing her to continue. Eventually, Margaret comes out of the house, smiling and holding a rubbish bag, and tells Jean Two that she's wanted inside.

A grotesquely funny sequence begins, as one woman after another runs out of the house clutching a plastic bag of rubbish which she puts in the dustbin. Each bag is bigger than the last, and each one has a label on it of a different kind of pet: 'puppy' for example, 'kitten', 'gerbil'. The women's actions are ludicrous, but perturbing because of the words that Margaret spoke inside the house: 'Please don't make me ... It can't breathe'. The final, and largest, bag is labelled 'dog'. Earlier, Jean Two has shown the audience a dog chew belonging to their dog, Rex. At the end of the rubbish-bag routine, she opens the skylight and calls 'Rexy ... Rex', then her glance lights on the dustbin and she closes the hatch. She comes out of the house, picks up the dog chew she held up earlier, lifts the dustbin lid and makes the noise of a bomb dropping as she slowly lowers the dog chew into the

Paper Walls, Scarlet Theatre Company. Performers: (left to right) Christine Entwisle, Jan Pearson and Joyce Henderson. Photo: Sheila Burnett

Paper Walls, Scarlet Theatre Company. Performer: Joyce Henderson. Photo: Sheila Burnett

bin. The sound is both aggressive and plaintive, a long-suppressed wail of anger and despair that has finally been given utterance, and, with it, something shifts. Previously Jean Two has been either a passive victim figure or a clown, jokingly papering over any cracks that appeared in the surface of normality the three women insistently presented. Now she goes into the house purposefully and closes the door behind her.

Music is heard from the house, and then a scream. Slowly, three dolls appear at the tiny window. Their beautifully-crafted faces are miniature replicas of those of the three women. The Jean-One doll is the first to appear, then the Margaret doll and the Jean-Two doll. They remain there, staring at the audience, and then the blind is pulled down. Lights flash in the darkness, there is the noise of a struggle and another scream. The house moves frantically, as if it is breathing, and the breath grows louder and louder until eventually it seems that the house must explode. There is the sound of one gunshot, then a second, and, after that, silence, stillness. In the darkness a faint noise begins, momentarily baffling, and then recognisable – the sound of someone sawing.

As the lights slowly come up, the tip of the gigantic saw Margaret demonstrated to the audience earlier is seen moving rhythmically down the front of the house, which is being methodically ripped apart. The sawing seems to take a long time, but it is a magic time. After the screams and the house's frantic breathing, the audience members slowly exhale their inheld breaths. When the saw has completed its work, fingers appear in the cracks, curling round the rough edges of the wood. Gently, almost tenderly, they open up the house ... and, inside, are all the tools they showed the audience earlier, hanging neatly on shelves. There is also the kettle that misted the window, so that one of the women could try to write on it a request for help, and a washing-up bowl containing the water that the two Jeans collected. It is the doll's house it originally seemed to be, with tools and cooking utensils all in their specially designated places.

The three women come towards the audience, and, addressing them as if they were first the police, and later a jury (or perhaps newspaper reporters), describe, and act out, what has taken place inside the house. It is a disgusting and horrifying story of daily humiliation and physical and sexual abuse by the man who has controlled every aspect of their lives: Jean One's husband, the father of Jean Two and Margaret. Every household task had to be performed to exact specifications that he laid down, and, if these specifications were infringed in any way, the culprit, or one of the other women was punished. The two Jeans demonstrate one such incident. Jean Two is doing the washing up, trying to do it soundlessly. Each time she makes a noise, her mother receives a blow. All three women, we learn, had to service the man's sexual needs, and wore wedding rings to signify that they were his 'wives'. They were forced to assist in the killing of

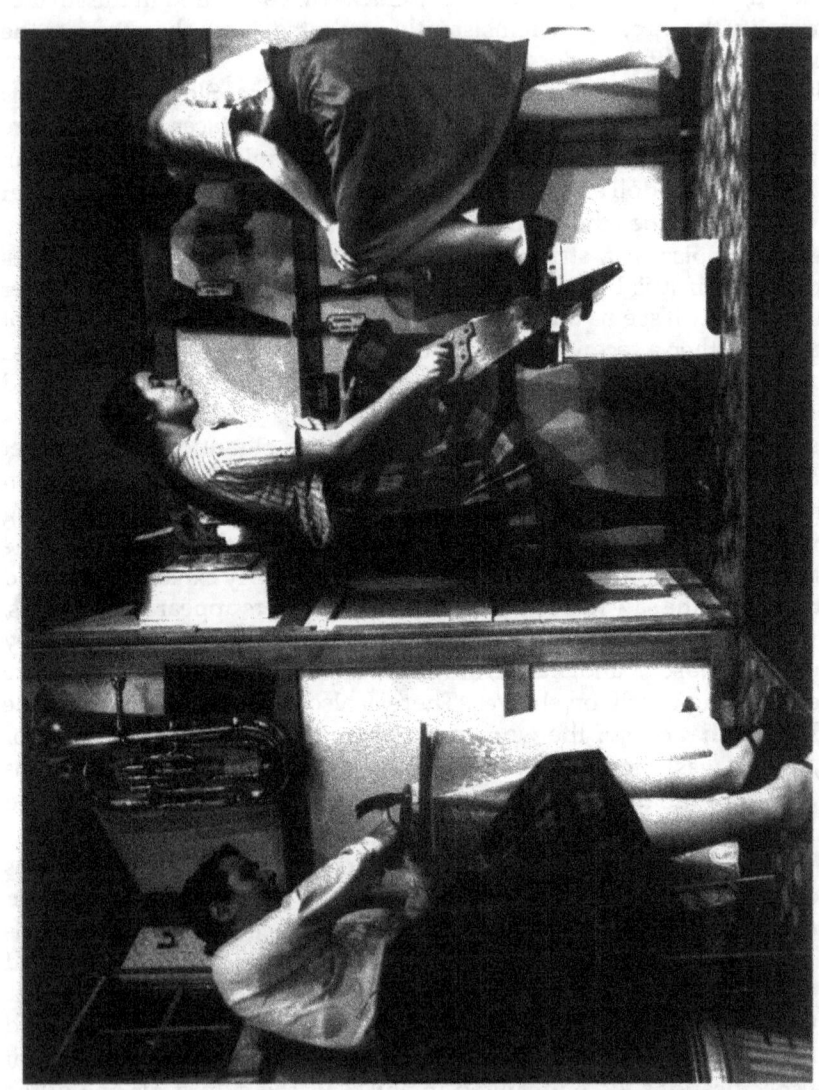

Paper Walls, Scarlet Theatre Company. Performers: (left to right) Jan Pearson, Christine Entwisle and Joyce Henderson. Photo: Sheila Burnett

household pets, were never allowed out of the house except to go to work, or to jumble sales to buy clothes. Trips to the B&Q, when supplies ran low for their prescribed DIY activities, had to be organised with military precision so that they could be completed before he returned home. At last, driven beyond endurance, they shot him, with the gun that was kept in case of burglars. There were two shots, and Margaret and Jean Two claim that they each shot him once. Their mother, they insist, was in the kitchen doing the washing up and was not involved.

In the second half of the piece, entities which were utilised by the man in the first half to imprison or degrade them are given new and liberating functions by the women. Their use of the gigantic saw to open up the house to view heralds this transformation. As big as the women themselves, the saw emphasises their previous diminutive status as dolls that the man could do what he liked with. When the saw opens the house, it is as if the dolls are taking revenge, and this idea is reinforced by the fact that the dolls' faces have been seen at the window just before the killing.

Near the end of the performance, the women bring the dolls close to the audience, and, holding them in front of their bodies, silently use them to demonstrate the details of the abuse they suffered. Jean Two sharply pulls her doll's hair, Jean One twists an arm of her doll behind its back, and Margaret slowly runs a finger down the inner leg of her doll, then lifts its skirt and places her hand underneath. Their actions suggest the responses of abused children, showing, through play, what they cannot fully articulate in words. The bodies of the large, exquisitely-made dolls replicate the pain and degradation the women suffered, and their still faces hauntingly reflect the frozen immobility of the faces of the three women holding them.

While the saw actively frees the women, water is used in the second half of the piece to celebrate that freedom. First, the women show the audience how water formed part of the systematic programme of torture to which they were subjected: Jean One is beaten every time Jean Two makes a mistake in her washing-up routine and Margaret is punished for breaking an egg by having water flung in her face. This is followed by a lyrical sequence in which the women undress as far as their petticoats, and Jean One washes her feet in a bowl of water. The three women sing together in harmony, the sweetness of their voices giving aural confirmation of the visual representation of the cleansing away of impurities and humiliations.

Like the saw and the water, the house – the women's prison – undergoes a transformation. During the killing of the man it appears to become disturbingly alive, struggling and gasping for breath as it totters precariously to and fro. When the death is replayed, this 'aliveness' takes on a new power: the house moves with deliberation first from side to side, then forward towards the audience as though it searches for, and eventually finds, a position in which it can settle.

The performance ends as (apart from the entrance of the man) it began, with a focus on the tiny four-paned window. The blind is drawn up, as it was at the beginning of the performance, but now the three women's faces are seen there, positioned as the dolls' faces were just before the killing. The women have taken the dolls' places. They open the window and look out. Whether they will be able to live in the world as sane adult human beings after what has happened to them is not clear, but the final moments of the performance are hopeful. The women breathe in the fresh air and begin to smile. Slowly, the lights fade.

Alice Power (co-director and co-designer) talking about Paper Walls

(*Paper Walls* was directed by two designers, Alice Power and Alice Purcell, each of whom had worked with Scarlet Theatre before. Alice Power designed *Our Age* and *Baby Baby*, and Alice Purcell designed *Vows* and *On Air*. *Paper Walls* was their first joint project for Scarlet Theatre and their initial venture as directors. In addition to directing, they also designed the set.)

The set: *As this was the first production we had directed, Alice Purcell and I wanted to be able to concentrate a large proportion of our energies on directing, rather than designing, and our initial intention was to have a set that one could virtually buy in a shop. The idea for the garden shed came from that need. At first we intended to buy a shed and adapt it, and then we realised that it would be cheaper to make it. We had the shed from the start of rehearsals and the show was built around it from the beginning. I think that's why the end product was so integrated. Usually in theatre you begin with an idea and then try to find the set that goes with it. The choice of a shed wasn't arbitrary, though. We saw it as a microcosm of a house, and we were interested in families, especially families that go wrong. Originally, we wanted to explore the idea of a family who believed that they were living in a grand house with a west and an east wing, while what the audience would see was the outside of a tool shed. So there was the domestic idea, and the sense of delusion, of things not being as they seemed.*

The rehearsal process: *There was a week of rehearsals when we played with the idea of the shed – its inside and outside, going into and coming out of the enclosed space. We didn't have any storyline, we were just looking at different characters. Then Alice Purcell brought in an article that she'd seen in a newspaper some time before. It was a story about abuse within a family, and, though we hadn't had any intention of working on abuse, the characters and events were so extraordinary that they captured our imaginations. The story also fitted very well with the idea of the house, and with another idea that we'd wanted to explore, which was that there was a problem that had to be solved. From the beginning we'd thought of problem-solving as a device to keep the piece running, and, in the article, the problem for the characters was the man (the abuser) whom they had to get rid of.*

Paper Walls, Scarlet Theatre Company, 1995 national tour. Performers: (left to right) Nicola Blackwell, Gráinne Byrne and Jane Guernier. Photo: Lietta Granato

Finding the article (especially at that point) was quite spooky because it confirmed things we'd been exploring anyway – DIY, for example – which featured in the article. We kept going back to the women's story in rehearsals, not in order to directly dramatise their lives, but, through exploring their extraordinary lifestyles, to examine the ways in which people became stuck in situations and consequently caught up in bizarre rituals and patterns.

We also had visual sessions in the rehearsals where members of the group (directors as well as actors) individually set up images that had the effect of photographs. For example, someone might be listening through the wall of the shed to what was going on inside. The image in Paper Walls of the giant saw slicing through the house came from one of these sessions. The shed had been positioned on its side, and the saw was sticking up through it. We had been thinking that the shed should open and close throughout the piece, but, once we'd established the idea of sawing it open, we realised that actually it only needed to open once and that it was much more powerful if the opening was delayed as long as possible.

The visual imagery sessions gave us a lot of material to work with. People have commented on the fact that you can sense the piece has been devised by designers, and I think that Alice and I being primarily visual artists was a crucial factor. We found images that we liked, and worked with these, rather than focusing on the psychology of the piece. Feelings and hunches about what we liked were all we had to go on really at the beginning. Then we had to keep digging and digging to find out what it was we were trying to do.

The dolls: Like the shed, and the idea of the malfunctioning family, the dolls were part of the work process from the beginning. We were able to create dolls that were miniature replicas of the actresses through a technique where you make a cast of a person's face and then shrink it. You use a special plaster which, in air, shrinks to about a third of its original size. Alice Purcell and I are both interested in puppets, and we also liked the idea of being able to change scale inside the house, especially given the fact that the house is the wrong scale anyway.

The work the actresses did with the dolls in rehearsal, looking after them and telling them their inmost thoughts that they kept hidden from everyone else, was very moving. It was also quite scary though, especially before we painted the dolls, when these copies of the actresses looked like sleeping spirits. It was like watching people in a dream state. Because dolls are used in helping children who've been abused to talk about their experiences, they also fitted in with the newspaper article, and this was another weird coincidence. Near the end of Paper Walls we did in fact use dolls as a way of revealing what had happened to the women. The characters showed the audience what took place, but, because they demonstrated it on the dolls, they remained to some degree outside events.

I suppose the dolls were both the characters, and external to them, though we didn't think about it in this way as we worked on it. At the time what we were interested in was layering images. Afterwards though the piece had its own logic.

The words: *Cindy Oswin came into rehearsals and watched us working and then we asked her to come up with bits of text. Sometimes in rehearsals she'd set something up and work with the actors herself. At other times she'd come in with maybe just a page of text and we'd work with that, changing the words where necessary and feeding things in from the actors. It was very to and fro. We also took bits of text from DIY manuals, especially one really old one.*

The music: *Nigel Piper had the same source material as we did in that he knew we were working on the shed, and he'd read the article and seen some of the rehearsals. He wrote three themes, one of which was particularly good. We used it at the beginning of the piece. It has sounds of domestic life, such as brushing, but it's also very musical. We didn't ask for these domestic sounds. They were Nigel's idea. He's a very intuitive artist. Once he'd established the theme, he developed a more disturbing, sinister version of it and a comical version for when the actors are doing DIY outside the shed. He also wrote music for the doll sequences.*

He was a very important part of the work process, and he was always willing to adapt what he'd composed. He would know from watching the piece in performance what was needed, and he kept on adding new bits. We even had a new piece for the performances at the South Bank. So, two years into its run, the show was till growing.

The humour: *You can never be sure how an audience will react but, ideally, in performance, the show is funny to begin with, and, then, as the audience gradually realise what is happening, there are moments when it is still funny, but in a weird way. I think it's very good if you can make people laugh and then think, "Oh dear, I shouldn't have been laughing". For me that's a good way into a serious subject because I wouldn't be interested in taking subject matter like that in* Paper Walls *and just making a serious piece about it. It was important to me to make a piece that, although it dealt with a an extremely difficult subject, still entertained people. I think the result was much stronger than a more agit-prop piece would have been because the audience had to work it out for themselves. They had to find the solution to the strange events on stage.*

Working on the domestic violence was horrible. It was a very difficult, very emotional experience, and I think every one of us was affected by it. The actors were trapped inside the shed for long periods, and the humour was very important to us in rehearsals as a way of getting through it all. It's a very fine line to tread, to try and make comedy out of such an unpleasant situation, but I think that's how comedy works. The most desperate situations are also the best comic situations.

Reactions to Paper Walls' success: *It was fantastic to be given the opportunity to direct, never having had any previous experience of directing, but Alice and I went into it without a sense of having much to lose personally. We felt a huge responsibility to the actors, but, though we really wanted to make the piece, we* didn't have high expectations for ourselves because it was all really so new. We talked about it for a long, long time before rehearsals began, and I think you lay your foundations by talking, without even knowing what these foundations are. It was a great experience, but I was surprised by how well received the show was. I watched it on the first night, and I thought, "What have we made?". It seemed to me it would be too difficult for people to cope with. At the time you're working you're too close to see it properly. You have to stop and stand back a bit to see it.

One really good lesson I've learned from the experience of working on Paper Walls is that there's no point in going in with particular expectations because it will turn out quite differently. I wanted to make a comedy, a funny show with women in it. We did make that, but we also made something else. You have to let it be what it is, not try to hang on to your original conception.

Performance Venues:

1994

18&19 February	Old Bull Arts Centre	Barnet
23 February	Clifton Arts Centre	Lytham St Annes
24 February	Padgate Campus Theatre	Warrington
1 March	Stahl Theatre	Oundle
2 March	Hind Leys, Shepshed	Loughborough
3 March	King Alfred's College	Winchester
4 March	Old Town Hall	Hemel Hempstead
8 March	Thames Valley University	Ealing
9 March	The Hawth	Crawley
10 March	Arts Centre	Eastbourne
11 March	Luton 33	Luton
12 March	Arts Centre	Peterborough
15 March	Borough Theatre	Abergavenny
17 March	Studio Theatre	Leeds
18 March	Queens Hall Arts Centre	Hexham
19 March	Buddle Arts Centre	Wallsend
20 March	Hebden Bridge Cinema	Nr Halifax

22 March	Unity Theatre	Liverpool
25 March	Arts Centre	Harrow
26 March	The Gantry	Southampton
5-30 April	New Grove, Drummonds	London

1995

9 August	Old Bull Arts Centre	Barnet
12 August-2 September	Assembly Rooms Fringe Festival	Edinburgh -
22 September	Dovecot Arts Centre	Stockton on Tees
23 September	Guildhall Arts Centre	Grantham
25 September	Exeter and Devon Arts Centre	Exeter
27&28 September	Arts Centre	Jersey
29 September	Forest Arts Centre	New Milton
30 September	Arts Centre	Colchester
2 October	John Leggott College	Scunthorpe
5 October	Northbrook Theatre	Worthing
6&7 October	Cambridge Drama Centre	Cambridge
10 October	South Holland Centre	Spalding
11 October	21 South Street	Reading
12 October	Pegasus Theatre	Oxford
13 October	Bowen West Theatre	Bedford
14 October	Portsmouth Arts Centre	Southsea
17-19 October	BAC	London
20&21 October	Unity Theatre	Liverpool
24 October	Jellicoe Theatre	Poole
25 October	Bournemouth University	Poole
26 October	Guildhall Arts Centre	Gloucester
27 October	Arts Centre	Rotherham

1996

22-24 January	Purcell Room South Bank Centre	London
1-3 February	West Yorkshire Playhouse	Leeds

Press Quotes

'Brilliant performers and an ingenious set-design by directors Alice Purcell and Alice Power ensure the work's theatricality never undermines its integrity.' (Clare Bayley, *The Independent*, 23 August 1995)

'a post-modernist masterpiece' (Bonnie Lee, *The Scotsman*, 18 August 1995)

'redefines the term "box set". Total theatre in miniature' (Keith Bruce, *The Herald*, 14 August 1995)

'But then you go to the breathtaking *Paper Walls* and come out soaring once more; for even one such play, yes, the three weeks are worth every hungover moment.' (Carol Sarler, 'Edinburgh Diary', *The Observer*, 20 August 1995)

2
FOURSIGHT THEATRE

Productions prior to *Boadicea: The Red-Bellied Queen* and *Slap*

1987/8 – *The Secret Vice*
1988/9 – *Mae West*
1989/90 *Hitler's Women*
1990 – *Mobs and Martyrs*
1990 – *Working Women of the Black Country*
1990 – *Helen*
1991 – *Working Women of the Black Country 2*
1991/2 – *Pink Smoke in the Vatican*
1992 – *Virgins and Whores*
1992/3 – *Shoot the Women First*
1993 – *Bloomers*
1993 – *Bloody Mary and the Virgin Queen*
1994 – *Frankenstein's Mothers*

Based in Wolverhampton, Foursight Theatre was set up in 1987 by four drama graduates from Exeter University with the intention of drawing on their common training background which centred on group creation. The majority of Foursight's productions to date have been based on stories of women in history. During the period of research for this book, the Joint Artistic Directors of Foursight were Kate Hale (a founder member of the company), and Sue Pendlebury.

Foursight Theatre defines its artistic policy as being to

- create new work.

- experiment with form and develop new skills.

- integrate textual/musical/visual/physical aspects of theatre.

- challenge the director/writer power base of mainstream theatre, by fully integrating the actor in the creative process.

- develop new, challenging ways of working with writers, choreographers, designers and composers within the creative process, whilst fully respecting the different needs of each art form.

- acknowledge that the quality of the experimental process is as important as, and directly informs, the quality of the product.
- encourage the realization of women's artistic creativity.
- apply the same process and exact the same standards in both their national touring and education work.
- encourage artistic collaborations with other companies and venues.
- make the work accessible both in terms of the performance and touring pattern of the work.
- develop new audiences.

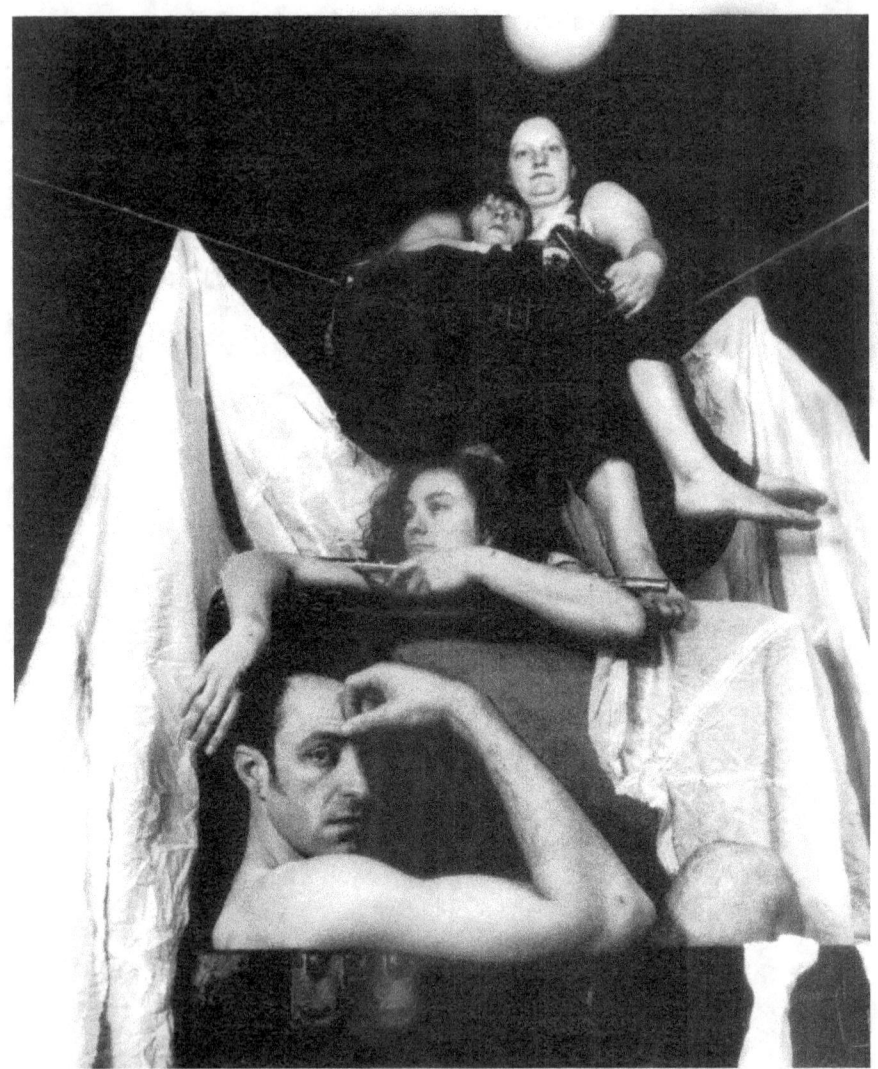

Boadicea: The Red-Bellied Queen, Foursight Theatre Company. Performers: (top to bottom) Stephanie Jacob as Boadicea, Sue Pendlebury as Voada, Katharine Ratcliff as Voddiccia and Simon Thorp as Marius. Photo: Des Gamble

Boadicea: The Red-Bellied Queen
(stimulus script by Cath Kilcoyne)

Credits

Boadicea	Stephanie Jacob
Marius/Suetonius	Simon Thorp
Voada	Sue Pendlebury
Voddiccia	Katharine Ratcliff
Directed by	Kate Hale
Movement Direction by	Kerry Ribchester
Music by	Jeff Corness
Designed by	Celia Forestal
Assistant Director	Deborah Barnard
Costumes	Sally O'Mara
Sign Teacher	Carole France
Front of House Photography	Des Gamble

Boadicea: The Red-Bellied Queen was based upon a narrative poem commissioned from writer, Cath Kilcoyne, and was created through a working process that aimed to utilise the specific skills of the director, writer, choreographer and composer, whilst also allowing the performers fully creative roles. An important source text for the devising process, and also for the following account of Boadicea's story, was Antonia Fraser's book, *Boadicea's Chariot: The Warrior Queens*.

Boadicea's Story

In the year AD 60 (or possibly 61) the Queen of a Celtic tribe called the Iceni led a revolt against the Romans who were occupying Britain. Known to history as Boadicea, her actual name is uncertain, though Tacitus gives it as Boudicca. Like her name, Boudicca's life story is open to speculation. Celtic culture was non-literate and the written version we have of her life comes therefore from non-Celtic sources (Tacitus and a second-century Greek named Dio Cassius).

The basic outline of Boudicca's life that emerges from their accounts is as follows: Boudicca was the widow of Prasutagus, ruler of 'a client-kingdom of Rome' (Fraser 1980: 46). In his will Prasutagus 'entrust[ed the] ... regency' (ibid.: 57) to his widow on behalf of two daughters (who were presumably not old enough as yet to rule in their own right). His 'land and personal possessions' (ibid.) he bequeathed in part to the Roman Emperor and in part to his widow to hold in trust for the daughters. This latter bequest was ignored by the local Roman officials, who seized the property in its entirety.

Perhaps as a result of some act of defiance (though, if so, Tacitus does not record this), Boudicca was flogged and her daughters raped.

Whether or not Boudicca engineered some form of rebellion prior to the assault on herself and her daughters, it is clear from Tacitus's writings that she did so afterwards, and on a massive scale. She gathered together a large Celtic army which she commanded in the destruction first of Camulodunum (Colchester) and then Londinium (London). Both places were lightly protected, if at all. At Camulodunum the Roman army veterans who were domiciled there attempted to repulse the Boudiccan army but were heavily outnumbered. While the sacking of Camulodunum was taking place Suetonius Paulinus, the Governor of Britain, was on the island of Mona (Anglesey) routing out and killing other Celtic rebels who had taken refuge there. When the news of the sacking of Camulodunum reached him, he moved his army swiftly towards Londinium, the next focus of Celtic attack. On arrival, however, he came to the conclusion that Londinium 'could not be defended' (ibid.: 82), and that, from a military point of view, the wisest course was to abandon it to its fate. In this way, Suetonius hoped to keep his forces fresh for a later assault on the Celtic army that might stand a greater chance of success. Following the departure of the Roman army, the Celts razed Londinium to the ground and butchered its remaining inhabitants. According to Dio Cassius, the atrocities they committed included cutting off the breasts of noblewomen and sewing them to their mouths.

Dio's account is uncorroborated and may therefore be an imaginary embellishment. The twentieth-century discovery, however, of a 'red layer ... of burned debris', 'approximately sixteen inches deep', situated 'about thirteen feet' beneath parts of what is now the City of London has borne witness to the severity of the Boudiccan attack (ibid.: 84). Fraser writes that the heat of the burning Londinium was comparable to the 'estimated heat of the firestorms in Hamburg during the 1943 bombings' (ibid.).

Suetonius's strategy of husbanding his forces until a more advantageous future moment paid handsome dividends for the Romans. The site of Boudicca's final battle is unknown, though there are various contenders, among them an area of the West Midlands near Nuneaton, and the neighbourhoods of two railway stations: King's Cross (London) and Virginia Water in Surrey. Whatever the site of the battle, its outcome for the Celts was bleak and devastating. Though numerically superior to the Romans, they were no match for their skilled professionalism. They were driven back, but found themselves unable to flee because they had brought their families with them to watch the battle and had positioned them in what they believed to be a safe place, behind the expected battle lines. When they tried to escape from the Roman advance, therefore, they found their way forward blocked. The Roman soldiers closed in on them and massacred everyone, warriors and their families. Even the baggage animals were butchered. In all, according to Tacitus, eighty thousand Celts perished, though only about four hundred Romans were killed.

Boudicca died (again according to Tacitus) by taking poison. What happened to her daughters is not recorded. Boudicca's burial site is unknown, though Stonehenge and 'a mound on Hampstead Heath known as Boadicea's tomb'(ibid.: 100) are among the places that have been mooted. The railway station motif continues in the suggestion that, if the area beneath Platform Eight at King's Cross were to be excavated, it would be found to contain Boudicca's remains.

Kate Hale (director) and Cath Kilcoyne (author of the stimulus script): reasons for choosing to work on the story of Boadicea

Starting points – Kate: *It was a story I'd always wanted to investigate because Boadicea is such a referred to historical figure. When I began to look at her in more detail, I was fascinated by the fact that her resistance to the Romans didn't consist of fighting them off on the cliffs of Dover. The Celts had already accepted a degree of Roman rule. So Boadicea's rebellion raises the issue of colonialism, and, interestingly, in this case, Britain was the victim of colonialism rather than the perpetrator of it. Then there was the fact that Boadicea had two daughters who were raped by the Romans, in a ritualistic way, as a political event. For me rape is an extreme version of the division between the sexes. I'm very interested in what it is that divides men and women, our sense of being part of a gender group. You go into schools and, regardless of whether the kids are black, or Asian, or white, even if they're very aware of the racial divide, if you ask them to sit down, they always sit in their gender, rather than their racial groupings. One is negotiating this gender divide every day in one's personal life, and, for me, rape is the cutting edge of that. War rape complicates the issue because in peacetime there are men who rape and men who don't. A decision is involved. Then, in war, things become confused, because so many men go down that path and the possibility of every man being a potential rapist becomes more of a question.*

Cath: *For me, the rape of the daughters was a very important starting point. When I begin to research historical material I need a reference point that will have relevance for today, and war rape (and also our eventual decision that one of the daughters should become pregnant as a result of that rape) had so many references, in Rwanda, for instance, and in Bosnia. A further aspect of Boadicea's story that I became very interested in was the divide between the Romans and the Celts. The powerful Roman civilisation considered the Celts to be barbarians, though in fact they had an ancient, established culture. There was little or no understanding of the other's perspective.*

Boadicea: The Red-Bellied Queen in performance

The action takes place in two locations, which are also two different time-scales: the Pastworld where events unfold chronologically, and the Netherworld in which the characters (who, in terms of the Pastworld, are now dead) try to understand what happened to them. In the Netherworld the 'Red-Bellied Queen' is called Boadicea and, in the Pastworld, Boudicca.

The performance begins in the Netherworld where reddish light reveals a tangled heap of bodies downstage centre. Music begins, urgent and anxiety-filled, and one of the bodies – the man, Marius – jerks upright. Cautiously, he checks that he is unobserved, then struggles to his feet and creeps over to a trunk upstage left, inside which he hides. Another figure, Voada, gets up and looks around anxiously. Voddiccia, Voada's sister, springs to her feet, runs upstage right, and grabs a pole with which to defend herself against any possible source of danger. She sees Voada, puts down the pole, and the two sisters hug each other, looking over their shoulders fearfully at the same time. Both are dressed in black T-shirts and leggings cut off at the knee. Over this outfit, Voada wears a brief pinafore dress in red tartan, Voddiccia a short skirt in the same material. Voddiccia's arms are ornamented with gold bangles. Both girls are dirty and ragged. On their feet are dusty boots. In silence, they move downstage and look at their mother, Boadicea, who is still lying on the ground. As they reach her she comes to life, raising her hands abruptly to her throat as though she is being choked. The sisters jump back in alarm and Boadicea gets to her feet. She is a large, powerful looking woman in a long, bedraggled tartan skirt. For the first time the characters speak.

> Voddiccia: Mother? I had to do it.
>
> Boadicea: Get away, I can't hear what you're saying, but get away. What's the matter with her?
>
> Voddiccia: She's saying we're dead.
>
> Marius: Don't shoot!
>
> Voddiccia: What's he doing here? Who brought him? Mother did you bring him? You always had to listen to him. Why did you bring him?
>
> Boadicea: I can't remember.

Voddiccia: Get out! What do you mean, private? Get up! Get out! Voada! He's mine, aren't you Marius?

Boadicea: Falling and falling, over and over. (*Boadicea*, unpublished script: 1)

The action that accompanies the words is jerky, almost puppet-like. Boadicea and Voddiccia rush upstage and each of them grabs a pole with which she briefly threatens the other. Voada, who is dumb, communicates with Voddiccia in sign language, and Voddiccia then translates this into speech for Boadicea's benefit. Next Voada crosses to the trunk and lifts up the lid, revealing Marius who raises his arms above his head as if afraid that someone is about to shoot him. Voddiccia goes over to the trunk and repeatedly lifts Marius up by the head, and then pushes him down again, so that he resembles an out-of-control Jack-in-the-box.

This brief opening sequence has introduced a number of the elements that will make up the narrative of Boadicea and her daughters, though neither they nor the audience yet grasp their significance. These elements – hostility between Boadicea and Voddiccia, Voada's dumbness and her pursuit of Marius, Marius's fear of being attacked and Voddiccia's desire to maltreat him – are then repeated twice, verbally and physically, each time in a briefer and more staccato form. For the characters, the repetition leads to the first dim stirrings of memory as fragments of their past lives begin to take shape in their minds.

There was a battle, Voddiccia reminds Boadicea, and a Roman general called Suetonius. Voada, who is pregnant and without a father for her unborn child, wants Marius to act as the father, but Boadicea vetoes that. They're not having a traitor in the family: the girls' father, Prasutagus, wouldn't have liked it. Voddiccia, who is sitting in the trunk, responds to these words by reverting to a little girl persona. In a high childish voice she claims that father wouldn't have liked any of it, and, anyway, if he hadn't died, none of the disasters that have taken place would have occurred. He'd have listened to her advice and now there wouldn't be a Roman left alive in the land. In addition, she would be Queen of the Iceni.

Her speech leads into a shrill little song about being Queen Voddiccia, in response to which the irate Boadicea slams the trunk lid down on her and sits on it. At first there is silence from inside the trunk, and Boadicea smiles, but then a faint voice is heard. Voddiccia is still doggedly singing her song. The trunk lid is lifted up, and, still childlike, but also now tearful, she sings of her desire to be reunited with her father. Boadicea brings Voada her violin and the lighting changes to a dark, sombre state.

Boadicea: The Red-Bellied Queen, Foursight Theatre Company. Performer: Katharine Ratcliff. Photo: Ian Griffiths

Pastworld

Funeral song and march, putting on of the torcs: The music Voada plays is haunting and elegaic. It wails and mourns, is permeated by the keening of women and the irreparable nature of loss. As Voada plays, Boudicca (as she is now called), and Voddiccia cover the trunk with a ceremonial cloth, and then carry it, held aloft like a funeral bier. Voada joins them and their voices blend in a wild incantatory lament.

When the music ends, Marius, positioned downstage centre right, addresses the audience as though they were the Iceni hordes. Unlike the rest of the Iceni, including Boudicca, he speaks Latin, and is therefore able to act as an interpreter of the Romans' intentions now that Prasutagus is dead. First, however, he explains carefully that he is 'merely a cipher for these negotiations', a 'spectator'. He 'take[s] no sides' (B.: 2) and hopes that his position as an impartial witness will be respected. What the Romans have to say through him is pithy and brutal. They do not accept the sovereignty of a woman. While Prasutagus was alive, they were willing to tolerate his status as client-king, but now they are placing the Iceni under direct rule. Boudicca is commanded to hand over 'all monies, weapons and sacred relics' (ibid.), including the Iceni insignia of royal command, the ceremonial necklaces known as the torcs. When Boudicca refuses to obey this command, and instead orders the Romans off her land, war is inevitable.

Panic: To the sound of urgent, anxiety-filled music, Voada and Marius perform a movement sequence suggestive of searching, Voada for safety and Marius for loot. He finds an Iceni bracelet in the trunk and puts it on. Voada positions herself on the trunk, from which she makes a flying leap on to Marius's back. She accuses him of stealing, but he tells her that he is looking after 'number one' (B.: 4), and advises her to do the same. The lighting changes so that the characters are lit from the front, as though by a searchlight which pinions them in the moment of arrested flight.

Rape and flogging: Boudicca's two daughters begin an orchestrated breathing sequence that signifies their rape by Roman soldiers. Voada stands centre stage, her arms above her head, wrists together as if tightly bound. Her body is taut, her eyes terrified. Her breath comes in long shuddering cries, as though it is being pressed out of her body by a great weight. Interwoven with the sounds she makes are those of her sister, harsh, sudden gaspings for breath. Boudicca is standing facing upstage, her body moving convulsively as though she is being flogged. Intermittently, she cries out in pain, while, at the same time, the actor who plays Marius crouches upstage and utters muted orgasmic groans that evoke the actions of the rapists. Voada falls to her knees and describes the rape of Voddiccia.

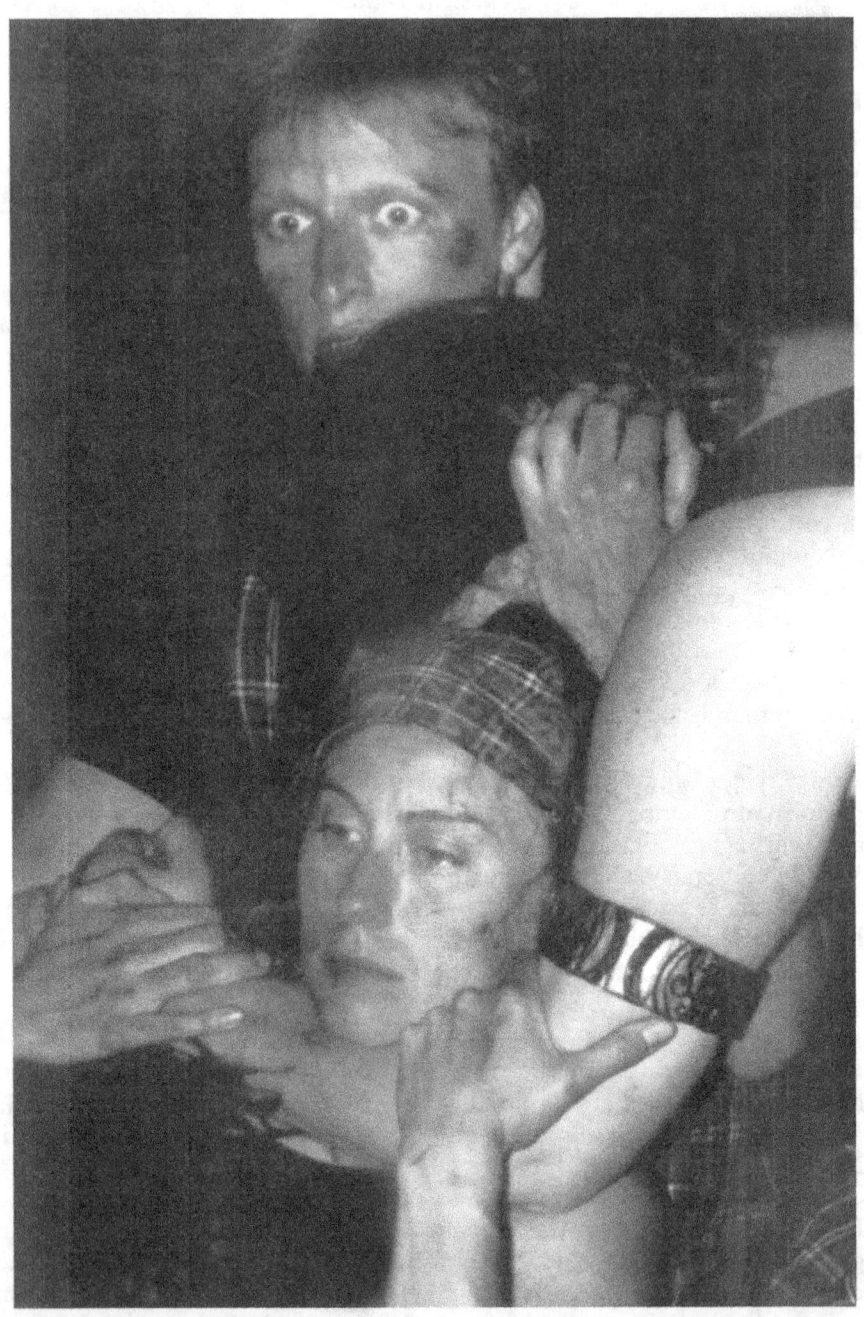

Boadicea: The Red-Bellied Queen, Foursight Theatre Company. Performers: (top to bottom) Sue Pendlebury, Stephanie Jacob and Katharine Ratcliff. Photo: Ian Griffiths

Voddiccia, my sister,
Voddiccia, the spear,
Caught,
Three men, four men, covering her face,
Hands bloody,
Spear her, spear her, spear her with their bodies.
One begins, one ends. Where? (ibid.)

During this, Voddiccia is lying on the ground, her body heaving and jack-knifing as she is violated. Her breathing changes to a cumulative sequence of frantic sniffing sounds, suggestive of lungs bursting, a nightmare feeling of weight, of being held immobile, and the presence of a vile and inescapable stink.

After the rape Marius goes to Voddiccia and picks her up gently, but she spits at him, wants to kill him, because he watched and did nothing. To protect himself, Marius offers to act as a spy for the Celts within the Roman camp. Boudicca accepts his offer, but warns him of what will happen to him if he fails to inform on his 'fat [Roman] masters'. 'We will come to you', she tells him, 'raw as we are now, blood in our mouths, and you will die' (B.: 5).

Netherworld

The lighting state changes to signify the Netherworld, and the characters return to the picking over of past events that they were engaged in at the beginning of the performance. Boadicea still finds it difficult to remember the details of what happened, but this failure of memory is partly wilful. She wants to tell the story in a manner that is most flattering to herself. As she is unable to read or write, Marius suggests that she should dictate her biography to him, and, when she gleefully agrees, they begin to compose the tale of 'The Red-Bellied Queen' – a 'Catchy title' (B.: 6), as Marius aptly remarks. In this version, the shocking immediacy of the rape that has occurred in the previous scene is muted and distanced through Boadicea's redefinition of it as a deflowering. In addition, Marius sanitises his own role in the events. Though Boadicea insists on calling him an informer, he writes down 'double agent' instead, and imagines himself heroically astride a 'pure white steed' (B.:7), instead of the terrified fugitive figure he actually was. At one point in this fabrication of the past Boadicea is assailed by doubts – should she perhaps have handed over the torcs to the Romans in order to protect her daughters, she wonders – but Marius tells her that doubts have no place in the story. If they must be expressed, they should be saved for the final chapter. Immediately, Boadicea re-envisions herself as a warrior queen. Doubts? What does Marius mean? In the final chapter she is victorious. Voddiccia snidely comments that she thought her mother claimed to be unable to remember what happened, but Boadicea is a match for her. She may not be able to recall the precise chronology of events, but she does remember the outcome. Triumphantly, she asserts that she won.

The mood throughout this section is comic. In the Netherworld the characters become grotesques, knock-about figures from a Punch-and-Judy world. Voddiccia does protest at the version of the past Boadicea and Marius are cobbling together, but her high, screechy tone of voice belies the importance of what she is saying. When she describes the rape the words she uses are horrifying, but they are delivered with ghoulish relish. Only Voada, who is dumb, retains a sense of the anguish of what happened. Through Voddiccia, who acts as her interpreter, she tries to offer her mother a different perspective on the rape One of the soldiers was crying as he did it, she tells her, but Boadicea dismisses this as irrelevant nonsense.

At Marius's instigation, Boadicea then transforms herself into an avenging goddess figure, and imagines herself addressing the Celtic war host before the sacking of Colchester. 'Time to avenge the bleeding sores of our daughters,' you declaimed, Marius prompts her, and, standing on the trunk upstage right, her daughters around her, Boadicea cries out for Roman blood. Her 'skin is alive with the insects of the plain! [Her] hair is spiked with bones! Rivers', she continues, 'spring where I piss!' (B.: 9). Her words, partly alarming, partly comic, are undercut by Voddiccia who suddenly remembers what really happened. It was not a time for eulogies, she tells her mother. They had to be silent because the place was 'crawling with Romans' (ibid.).

Pastworld

Colchester, preparation for the battle: In dim light the characters cross and recross the stage, always watching for signs of danger. As they move, they play snatches of music on various instruments, and their voices likewise weave an intermittent sound texture: Voddiccia's joy at the prospect of revenge, Boudicca's ordering of Marius into Colchester to instil fear into the enemy, and his obedient 'Whispers of a coming doom' (B.: 10). Their words lead into the singing of a battle hymn to Andarte, the war goddess, Boudicca standing flanked by her daughters, with Marius behind her.

> Andarte!
> I will give you blood to bathe in.
> Heads to dangle in your ears.
> I'll give you human skin to clothe your body.
> Andarte! Andarte! (ibid.)

Boadicea: The Red-Bellied Queen, Foursight Theatre Company. Performers: (left to right) Simon Thorp, Stephanie Jacob, Sue Pendlebury, with Katharine Ratcliff balanced on poles. Photo: Ian Griffiths

On Boudicca's subsequent cry of 'Time!', the battle begins. There is the noise of drumming, and the characters move swiftly into a line downstage, facing the audience. Repeatedly, they mime gestures of war, taking imaginary arrows from pouches on their backs, for example, fixing them into bows and putting them into flight. Next, they run upstage right, collect the poles that are positioned there and form them into a moving sequence of supporting bars and obstacles upon, and through, which Voddiccia balances and summersaults.

Boudicca then loudly and triumphantly describes the destruction of Colchester and its inhabitants. This is followed by a blackout and, in the darkness, Boudicca is heard singing very softly:

And we will rise, Iceni,
So let them come and let them die.
We will not rest till freedom stands
In the sacred groves of Britain's lands. (ibid.)

Light gradually picks out her face and figure, then that of the others as they join her in song. The mood is fervent, yet reverent. This is not the exultation of battle but rather a holy fixity of purpose.

The lights come up sharply and there is an immediate change of atmosphere as the women listen to Marius's contemptuous description of the stunned response of the Roman general to the news of the sacking of Colchester. His words paint the general as a buffoon worsted by the superior strength of 'Boudicca, the warrior wench, the barbarian babe, the red-bellied Queen' (B.: 11), but eventually he admits the truth: ten thousand Romans are two days' ride away, and the general is spoiling for revenge.

The Life-stone: From the trunk, Boudicca gets the ceremonial cloth, which she lays on the ground, stage right, and upon which she places the life-stone. Voddiccia kneels behind it, low to the ground, then, behind her, Voada, whose upper body remains erect. Boudicca stands behind them. The lighting is dim and soft, as Boudicca first speaks and then, together with her daughters, sings an invocation to Andarte (the war, and also the mother goddess). The quality of the sound is lyrical and prayerful, but the words chill the blood. '[S]trip away the shreds of my mercy', Boudicca implores. 'Destroy my mother heart, so I can avenge my children' (B.: 12). The song's chorus repeats the promise the Iceni made before the Colchester battle: they will reward the goddess with human heads and skin if she grants them victory. Now, however, the words frighten Voada, who asks for an explanation of what is happening. Voddiccia tells her that the life-stone has absorbed Boudicca's remnants of weakness so that she will now be able to fight the next, and crucial, battle remorselessly. Voada however knows differently. The life-stone is full of love, and she no longer feels able to call the avenging fury that Boudicca has become mother. She does not want to fight.

London Battle: Boudicca and her daughters collect large flags and take up positions upstage centre. Voada, holding a tattered Union Jack, stands on the trunk. On each side of her, Boudicca and Voddiccia wield large red flags, signifying the presence of the Iceni. As Marius keeps up a persistent drumming, they whirl the flags around their bodies and swirl them through the air in a show of military might. The Iceni have reached London, but can find no trace of the reputed ten thousand Roman soldiers. Instead there are only women and old men. 'Kill them anyway' (ibid.), Voddiccia cries, and she and Boudicca begin to pace to and fro, surveying the intended victims. Meanwhile, Voada, who has put down her flag, plays her violin in an attempt to drown out their words. Boudicca focuses on a group of women prisoners. 'Don't cry', she tells them (B.: 13). Crying is useless because she is without mercy. Their sons raped her daughters, therefore the mothers are no longer women, but 'flesh bags, ready for the splitting'. 'Cut off their breasts', she orders. 'Terrible to think your breasts suckled such monsters .... It's your turn to suckle now .... Sew them [the breasts] to their lips' (ibid.). Voddiccia mimes this action, her face simultaneously that of a child and a torturer, and Voada tries to speak, to stop what is happening, but discovers that she no longer has a voice. As the Roman women's bodies are mutilated, their screams silenced, Voada's lips simultaneously become sealed.

Netherworld

In the Netherworld Boadicea, Voddiccia and Marius immediately forget the immediacy and horror of what took place, but, even more strongly than before, Voada holds fast to memory. Bereft of speech, she articulates her feelings through the voice of her violin, which sobs out a reprise of the funeral song that ushered the characters' first entry into the Pastworld. Determined to restore a feeling of lightness, Boadicea collects her accordion and begins to play a jig, instructing Voddiccia and Marius to join in. The jolly music captures Voada's attention briefly and she begins to play the jig too, but then she remembers what happened at the London Battle, and, briefly, she refinds her voice in order to tell Boadicea an admonitory story called 'Big Stone and Little Stone'. First she holds up the life-stone, which she names Big Stone. This represents her mother. Next, she demonstrates a smaller stone, Little Stone. This is herself. One day, so her story goes, Big Stone and Little Stone went for a walk in the forest where they saw spiders spinning their webs. Big Stone didn't like spiders, so she cut off their heads and pulled off their legs. Little Stone, who had once been 'attacked by a spider', joined in, though she didn't 'see the point of it'. Big Stone grew bigger and bigger 'until she crush[ed] everything in the forest. Little Stone [was] speechless with horror' (B.: 14). The next day she laid an egg, which hatched to reveal a spider.

Voada's story contains two vital messages, both of which Boadicea refuses to take heed of. The first is that Voada is pregnant by the enemy. Like Little Stone, she will give birth to what her mother hates and fears. The second is that Boadicea has become the thing that she hates. Her killing of the loathed spider (the Romans) has transformed her into a monster of destruction.

Grumpily, Boadicea gets into the trunk in order to disassociate herself from Voada's words. In her hand she holds the book in which she is creating her version of the past. 'There's nothing there about the torture', Voada accuses, grabbing the book from Boadicea. 'It's all lies, omissions and fantasy' (B.: 15), but Boadicea laughs at her and Voada returns to her former state of dumbness. Now that she is silent once more, the atmosphere changes, becoming first flippant, then grotesque. Together, Boadicea and Voddiccia sing a jaunty, but ghastly, little ditty about the mutilation of the London women:

>Boadicea: What a breast, what a breast, what an east and west!
>Blimey what a breast she's got
>I cut it off,
>
>Voddiccia: I sewed it on.
>
>Boadicea: Hanging from her mouth like a little cherry bun!
>What a knocker!
>
>Voddiccia: What a shocker!
>
>Both: Oh my we did laugh!
>
>Boadicea: If you want a titter, then nothing could be fitter.
>We'll do her other half. (B.: 16)

At the end of the song, they call out to Suetonius to come and view the results of their handiwork. Without warning, characters and audience are plunged into darkness – and into the Pastworld.

Pastworld

The killing of Marius: Voddiccia tries to pursuade her mother to mount a surprise attack on the Romans, but Boudicca points out that they don't yet know where the enemy is. They need intelligence from Marius. Marius however has failed in his task as an informer. He is unable to give them any information as to the Roman position, and Boudicca, believing that he has sided with the Romans, and that a traitor who doesn't do his job is worthless, allows Voddiccia to kill him. In a simulated replay of what was done to her when she was raped, Voddiccia forces Marius to the ground, and, sitting astride him, alternately punches and slaps him, and mimes repeated sexual intercourse. 'I'm not afraid of Romans' (B.:17), she calls out frantically, continuing to ride and hit him. Finally she kicks him away, and, trembling all over, calls out in a thin high wail, 'Mother, Mother' (ibid.)

The Baby: Voada goes to Voddiccia to comfort her and Voddiccia begs Voada to speak. Instead, Voada signs to Voddiccia, who translates her words into speech for their mother's benefit. When Boudicca and Voddiccia tortured the Roman women, Voada explains, the baby inside her stole her voice. But, though dumb, she can foretell the future. The Iceni will lose the battle. The goddess, Andarte, has warned her of this. Every blow they strike against the Romans is in reality a blow against themselves. If they want to kill every Roman, they will have to kill her because she is carrying a Roman baby.

Accompanied on the flute by Voddiccia, Voada then performs 'The Baby Dance', which begins gently and tenderly, then transforms into a frenzied re-enactment of her experience of rape. As though she is being pulled up by the hair, Voada rises on to her toes, her body rigid with fear. In the next sequence of the dance, she moves to Marius, who is lying on the floor, drags him upright and softly touches his face. Though he is larger and heavier than she is, she lifts and carries him. Previously the desired father of her child, he is now the child itself. Carefully, she lowers him back to the ground.

The Conjuring up of Suetonius: Together, Voddiccia and Boudicca lift the body of Marius and place him in a sitting position on the trunk. Boudicca needs to know the whereabouts of Suetonius, the Roman general, in order to plan her future strategy, but she is also fascinated by Suetonius as a man. In order to find out more about this 'reservoir of power' (B.: 19) she begins to transform the dead Marius into Suetonius. As the lights narrow in focus so that only Boudicca and the still figure of the man are illuminated, she collects a laurel wreath and places it on Marius/Suetonius's head. She arranges one of his hands so that it appears to hold a glass of wine, and breathes on his 'Roman cheek' (ibid.), infusing life into him so that she will be able to hear the texture and timbre of his voice. 'You can 'smile at me', she tells him, 'call me a Celtic hag queen whore' (ibid.). This doesn't matter. She wants to see him, to know what colour his eyes are. At this, Marius's, now Suetonius's, eyes dart open, but he ignores Boudicca. Instead, he preens himself, licking his fingers and arrogantly miming putting on mascara. He has no personal interest in Boudicca or any of the Celts. He is in Britain

Boadicea: The Red-Bellied Queen, Foursight Theatre Company. Performers: Stephanie Jacob (left) and Sue Pendlebury. Photo: Des Gamble

Boadicea: The Red-Bellied Queen, Foursight Theatre Company. Performers: Sue Pendlebury (left) and Katharine Ratcliff. Photo: Des Gamble

simply because he has been allocated this 'Damp. Disorganized. Rather dreary' little island as his province (ibid.). The Celts will thank the Romans, however, he claims, in the long run. Think what their descendants will be getting: 'good straight roads, baths, decent architecture, sublime literature' (B.: 20).

Rival Prophecies: Alternately, point by point, Boudicca and Suetonius address their armies, facing out to the audience as they do so. This is the enemy, Boudicca tells her warriors contemptuously, 'a man in a skirt and mascara' (ibid.) She reminds them of the mother goddess of war – Andarte – who is not yet satisfied despite the Roman blood she has drunk. In the coming battle the Iceni will be victorious, she promises, and they will push the parasites that have sought to devour them back to Rome. While Boudicca's words are hot and fierce, Suetonius's are cold and remorseless, like the Roman army he commands. In his own eyes, Suetonius represents order and implacable determination in the face of impassioned, yet chaotic force. A man of ice, he will defeat what he sees as the woman of rage and blood.

Netherworld

'Right, that's that then', Boadicea begins. 'We all know what happens next.' Write it down in the book, she orders Marius, 'the final chapter. "The big battle – how I won!"' (ibid.). Voada goes to Marius to take off his crown, but he is still in his Suetonius role and he prevents her. As Boadicea continues to declaim her version of the final battle, echoed by Voddiccia, Suetonius walks – remote, yet power-filled - around the stage. When he reaches centre stage, Boadicea and Voddiccia begin to circle him, still narrating their battle paean, but, as Boadicea reaches the climax of her story, Voddiccia remembers the real course of events: the Celts charged, yelling and screaming downhill to where the Romans had formed an 'invincible arrowhead' (B.: 21). Their spears were met by a wall of shields and then, when they were defenceless, the Romans butchered them with their short swords that were so ideal for hand-to-hand combat. The Celts turned and ran, back the way they had come from, but they had brought their families to watch the battle, leaving them protected, as they thought, behind the assault force. As the warriors' chariots were overturned, Celt after Celt was crushed by their own wagons and screaming horses. Hemmed in on all sides, they 'ran, tripping and stumbling, weak and frightened, eighty thousand Celts, a sea of Celtic blood, a massacre' (ibid.).

Throughout Voddiccia's speech Marius repeats his before-battle oration, while Voada plays a keening dirge on the violin, and Boadicea repeats stabbing and tearing motions from the Colchester and London battle sequences. At the end of the speech, Boadicea falls to the ground, gets up, falls to the ground. 'Falling, falling, falling. Over and over', she says (ibid.). With her flute, Voddiccia mimes cutting Boadicea's throat: 'I had to do it. Mother, Mother' (ibid.). Slowly, Boadicea gets to her feet once more, moves to upstage right and stands with her back to the audience, but looking back towards Voddiccia who now sits centre stage, facing stage left – lost, defeated. Marius/Suetonius takes off his laurel wreath and moves upstage, where he then sits. The lights focus on Voada, standing on the trunk centre stage, playing her anguished, achingly sweet lament. Her face is fixed, expressionless. The lights dim to blackout, and the last, faint stirrings of the music are heard. SILENCE.

Kate Hale and Cath Kilcoyne: the rehearsal process

Kate: *Once Sue (Sue Pendlebury, Joint Artistic Director of Foursight Theatre) and I had decided to work on Boadicea's story, Cath and I spent a lot of time talking about possible structures, and developments to the narrative. As the story was complicated, and there were a number of characters involved, we felt that we had to start from a brief and what we came up with was a triangular character structure. Boadicea was at the top and the two daughters, Voddiccia and Voada, were at each side. Through the daughters, we wanted to explore polarised reactions to rape. One daughter would become brutalised emotionally, and would react in a brazen and overtly sexual way, while the other would lose her voice and turn inward.*

We were also auditioning actors at this point and, with the decision as to who would be playing the parts, came the idea that Boadicea would be primarily verbal, Voada physical, and Voddiccia physical and verbal. In the middle of the triangle was the man, whom we named Marius, and we were thinking of the different identities that 'man' represented for the three women. Our intention at that point was that, for Voada, he would be the rapist, and the father of her child. For Boadicea, he was a competitor and a fellow warrior, and, for Voddiccia, a lover (though, because of her experience of rape, a lover in a warped sense of the word). Cath's brief from this point was to come up with an imaginative chronology, because there were so many holes in the narrative, so many decisions to make about the characters before everyone came together for the devising process.

Cath: *What I wrote was a stimulus script in the form of a poem. A stimulus script isn't like a finished piece of art work. What you're trying to do is to maximise potential for discussion, to provide stimulus for dramatic exploration. You're throwing up possibilities for a creative brainstorm. If one was writing a play, it would be necessary to be much more careful and perfectionist, but here you're trying to give lots of different ideas that can be picked up and developed.*

Kate: *When the actors came together at the start of rehearsals, we spent the first week working on movement with Kerry (the choreographer). The second week was spent discussing the stimulus poem. Cath came up that week and read it through with us and gave us her point of view. There was a lot of debate about what we wanted structurally, and what we didn't. The two worlds that we create in the production (the Pastworld and the Netherworld) were in my head at that stage as a possible starting point, and I put forward the idea that we should start the play after death. At that point I didn't know whether we'd alternate between the worlds (as in fact we do) or simply have a beginning scene in the Netherworld and a concluding scene that would take place there after death. The reason for having the two worlds was to bring a different perspective to bear on the material. I wanted the Netherworld to take a more objective view of events, and I also wanted it to be funny because, otherwise, the piece could easily become intense to the point where it would be unbearable. It's very important to provide a way in for an audience who are coming from daily life. You can't expect them suddenly to respond with the same kind of intensity that we would feel after three months' work.*

In a number of ways The Red-Bellied Queen was a new departure for Foursight Theatre. It was the first time they'd worked with a choreographer and a musical director, and also the first time they'd employed a male actor – *Kate*: *Looking back, I don't think it was an accident that the original four people who formed Foursight Theatre were women, given who we were. I think that actually we wanted to work with women, but we didn't make a conscious decision to do this. Instead, we chose to work together and **then** became conscious of the fact that we were all women.*

*Once we'd formed the company, we had to think of ourselves as a women's theatre company by virtue of the fact that that was how we were treated. Given the political situation of Britain at that time a group of four women working together was inevitably perceived as a women's company (in contrast to four men who wouldn't necessarily be seen as a men's company). So there wasn't really any argument. We **were** a women's company whether we liked it or not. The question of whether we should only employ women or not simply didn't arise in the early years because we found it difficult enough to keep ourselves going.*

When we became more established, we thought that, as it was obviously clear to everyone else that we were a women's company, we should go with that image. So, we employed women writers. In fact, we have also employed men occasionally, as designers, set constructors, workshop leaders. We've never been totally separatist. When it came to this production, Sue and I were discussing who the fourth character should be, and it suddenly came to me that it needed to be a man, because the Roman world that the women were reacting to is so male. I felt that, if we didn't have a man, we'd get to the point where the play would struggle. We needed the sense of a male military presence. The fact that the father of Voada and Voddiccia has just died at the start of the play is also significant.

Cath: *It seems to me that employing a male actor is an important move for the company to be making at this point, partly because there's a limit to the debate you can have without the presence of a man, and also because, in a wider feminist context, the focus is, I think, on men exploring for themselves, and entering into a debate with feminists about their own attitudes to various issues.*

There was the danger, though, that the male onstage would be scapegoated in some way. I know we wanted to explore scapegoating, but there remained the question of whether to make the man – and that particular man – the scapegoat. It's a question really of what options he has. I was thinking, for example, of the position of people in occupied France in the Second World War, or in the recently dismembered Eastern Block. What choices did they have? For Marius, it's a question of whether to side with the Romans, and, then, what happens at the point where you come face to face with the level of your betrayal (if it can be called that). What do you do? Can you turn it back? Ultimately you can't. That's what interested me in the character of Marius. I always question myself: "If I was living in this situation, would I collaborate? And, if so, how far?" By dint of silence, are you collaborating? After the rape, Voddiccia accuses Marius by saying, 'You did nothing. You watched. You saw it.' What does doing nothing mean?

Kate: *How valid a defence is his 'They'd have killed me'? There's also the fact that Boadicea uses him. She doesn't make her decision that he should die because he doesn't intervene. She capitalises on his essentially amoral nature and uses him for her own ends, then, when he's no longer useful, she allows him to be killed by Voddiccia.*

Along with the very male-orientated Romans, we also wanted to explore women's violence, and taking responsibility for that violence. If you're going to release violence, you have to take responsibility for it. As a company we've never been very interested in presenting good roles for women. We're far more interested in exploring the nooks and crannies that maybe women don't want to look at - consciously delving into the darker side, though in a positive way.

Analysing the work process: Kerrry Ribchester and Jeff Corness

Kerry Ribchester (choreographer): *In the past five years of working with physical theatre companies I've found that Body-Mind Centering and Physical Integration techniques help actors to focus and become more fully engaged in their bodies and movement. They deepen the quality of their movement and enrich the emotional journeys of their characters. Body-Mind Centering focuses on the major body systems, accessing specific organs, glands, nerves, fluids, bones and muscles. In this way it utilises the body's inner resources toward a greater emotional and physical expression.*

During the first week of rehearsals we did a lot of body work on the organs. Working on the liver was particularly useful in releasing a forceful energy, perfect for fuelling improvisations on war.

I also placed a lot of emphasis on the spine and pelvis to really ground everyone. The Red-Bellied Queen is a very demanding piece of theatre, and it's important that the performers are physically grounded and emotionally present. It is, in addition, a deeply emotive and impassioned piece, and I became very engaged with the ideas we were exploring. The Celtic women were extremely powerful. They inherited land and fought. It was my vision that the performers would embody this strength and depth through their physicality. For example, it was important to establish the power of the spine emanating through the front of the body.

The three-dimensional depth from moving with a greater awareness of the organs gave an earthy quality and supported the gestures, turns, lifts, and vocalizations. Stimulating the synovial fluid in the joints created a great sense of balance and the ability to move quickly without effort.

The actions of the Celtic women were so full of courage and I found myself speculating about what Boadicea would think if she were to come back now and see the ways in which women are still being abused, in Bosnia for instance. For me it's important that Voddiccia vents her anger about what has happened to her. In a women's theatre company we need to be seen to be dealing with the ugly side, the anger that to a large extent women keep within their bodies, because our culture doesn't allow women to release it. Anger is seen as 'working class', or 'ugly'. I think it's very important that the play gives vent to that emotion.

Jeff Corness (composer): *From the beginning I was very interested in the dichotomy between the Romans and the Celts, and the issues of colonialism it raises. In Canada now, where I live, we're embroiled in a debate about land claims. When the British arrived in Canada they had no idea how to make sense of the culture they found there. They couldn't understand the economic system at all. They couldn't see that the potlatches were an integral part of the native system. To the British colonialists they seemed to be simply a terrible waste of resources that left the people poverty stricken, and so they banned them. They also failed to grasp the native view that it's impossible to own land, or a river. It was like the divide between the Romans and the Celts. Neither culture could understand the other.*

Before rehearsals started I read Cath's stimulus poem, which I found very exciting. It made me think of some of the passionate, percussive rhythms that I'm interested in exploring in my personal music. Then, when the piece had been cast, I received details of the instruments the performers played – accordion, flute, clarinet, violin – and it was a far cry from the percussive element I'd had in mind!

For the first two or three weeks of rehearsals, it wasn't at all clear to me what the tone of the piece was going to be. Was the main focus on the Netherworld, or were we going to be telling the story as Cath had told it in her poem? Was it going to be distanced and ironic, or passionate and emotional? Gradually, as the piece began to come together, I realised that the first pieces of music I'd written didn't fit. So it was a matter of continuing with the search, trying to avoid the classic pitfalls when you're using tape, especially the danger of music overpowering what's happening on stage.

I was very conscious of trying to find a foundation from which to launch the musical elements. I was fascinated by the struggle of the Iceni, and I developed what I would call 'anthemic' music – for the Colchester sequence for example. There is also spooky movie music, which is used to underscore the action or atmosphere. Because we use such a lot of music in the show we're also able to use silence as a musical element.

The performers: their backgrounds and reasons for wanting to work on Boadicea

Stephanie Jacob (Boadicea): My background is that I did an English degree and then trained as a teacher for a year. Following that I worked for five years in Theatre-in-Education. For the last six or seven years I've been working in rep. and as a touring actor. I wanted to do this project for two reasons. The first was that I wanted to work with Kate, partly because she's a good friend, but also because she's a woman director, and in all my professional experience to date I've never been directed by a woman. Some of the male directors I've worked with have had problems with strong women and I wanted to feel that my ideas would be welcome in the rehearsal room. The second reason was that I've felt unchallenged doing rep. work. This is not a criticism of the places I've worked at so much as a criticism of the times. I think people are very careful about what they put on now. They don't feel able to take risks and I wanted to do something risky.

When I first came into the rehearsal room, though, I felt worried that I didn't have the necessary background for the work. The others were all used to working as physical theatre performers, and I didn't have that kind of training. I was thinking, "What can I offer?". I felt that there were huge opportunities, but I wasn't sure how I could contribute and I hoped that, at some point, words would be valuable.

Katharine Ratcliff (Voddiccia): Until last October I was working with a theatre company, Might and Main Productions, that I'd founded with two friends five years earlier. I'd come to feel that I needed some fresh creative input. Creatively, I'd reached a cul-de-sac within that structure, and I was also very tired from all the administration. I was keen to be just a performer in a show rather than always having to take on some form of directorial role as well. My experience has been with physically-based, devised work, and so, when I heard about this job, I auditioned to find out more about it.

Simon Thorp (Marius/Suetonius): My background in the last six years has been touring with physical theatre companies, primarily Volcano Theatre and I 0 U. I also had my own company for a while, The Wilde Players. I 0 U Theatre offered me a job at the same time as I was offered this job, and I had to choose between them. In the case of I 0 U I already knew and trusted the group, whereas the Foursight Theatre job would mean working with a group of complete strangers. So it wasn't a decision I rushed into. I eventually decided to do this job because I felt that it would push me more. I knew that there would be a long devising process, and in the last few years I haven't been involved in devising. I've mostly worked with directors who've created a text and then we've worked on it in a traditional way. The rehearsal period has been short. The Foursight Theatre job was the opposite of this: an eight-week devising process in which we would create our own text and characters. Also, in the I O U job I would have been silent, and I like speaking on stage. So I took this job because it presented the greater challenge.

Sue Pendlebury (Voada): *I joined Foursight Theatre in 1994 because I wanted to be able to pursue my physical theatre work, and because I would then have some control over what physical material I could explore. The physical and musical aspects were important to me and Foursight was able to give me a platform to pursue them. The first show I worked on with Foursight* (Frankenstein's Mothers) *incorporated quite a lot of music, and I wanted to build on that, and also on the use of physical movement in* Boadicea. *We have three physical performers in this production who are also musicians, and a performer with a very strong language background. I wanted to integrate all these different elements into a form of total theatre.*

Cath Kilcoyne's poem as a stimulus for the devising process

Stephanie: *I found Cath's stimulus poem a very useful impetus into devising. Normally, with devising, you're working from research material, which you hope will provide you with a character. I've based characters, for example, on people I've interviewed, or sometimes a tiny incident that I've read about. It was very interesting reacting off a character in a poem. Sometimes I disagreed with the way Cath had chosen to present points. They didn't fit in with my, admittedly very basic, historical reading. For example, when the daughters are raped, Boadicea, in the poem, reacted by cutting off the head of one of the rapists. I felt that this was wrong, that she should be passive and just have to bear witness to the event. For her as a mother this creates a profound sense of guilt which helps to explain the revenge she later takes on the Romans. It was very interesting to have the poem as a stimulus because of the way it helped us to shape choices about the characters.*

Katharine: *The poem was very valuable in helping us to develop the narrative. There was a lengthy process at the start of the devising process which was just discussion. We talked and talked about what happened and when exactly certain realizations should occur. When we got that clear we began to do big, long, loose improvisations about the Pastworld.*

Stephanie: *There's a tiny, but lovely thread in the poem about Boadicea's increasing fascination with Suetonius. It's only a couple of lines, but they developed eventually* into the creating of Suetonius. Kate set up an improvisation in which she asked me to conjure up Suetonius, and this provided some very interesting material, which we pursued. I found the improvisation stage fascinating because it was such a valuable flowing together of ideas. The poem was linguistically rich and had been very carefully thought about by Cath, and the characters were beginning to blossom at this stage. So, what was happening was the meeting of these two elements, and Kate seeing possibilities, and creating structures from their interrelation.

Responses to the rape, and to the ending of Boadicea

Katharine: *Awful as the rape is for the daughters and Boadicea, it's also symbolic of much more. The entire tribe is dispossessed and a whole way of life is threatened with destruction.*

Stephanie: *It seems to me that both Voada's and Voddiccia's stories add up to much more than that particular moment when they're held in such stark contrast – that single decision to be dumb or to be vicious. We have struggled throughout the devising process to place different elements of the various characters, in order to contribute to all the things an audience might feel. I was very impressed by people's integrity in working on the material, by their not saying that what happened is unimaginable, but really trying to use their imaginations to put themselves through those events. One problem is that we come to the story with a twentieth-century humanity that might not have been relevant, or possible, then. We do know, though, that some people survived the worst of those times, so, in a sense, the characters are survivors, as well as everything else. I really wanted that to come across, that Boadicea is a survivor in a way. She may be limbless, but she keeps going, and that's a true thing too about women.*

Sue: *I hope that, when I play the violin at the end of the play, there is a sense of hopefulness. It's as though Voada has found something beyond being able to talk. I'm clinging on to the life-stone just before I play, and, for me, as Voada, this represents love. Voada has a choice (regardless of whether she will actually live to have the child) to see it either as something negative and destructive, or as something that she actually wants. Because of the child she is carrying, she represents the possible joining of forces, the living together of the Celts and the Romans. I felt that for Voada as a character it was important that she shouldn't want to get rid of the child, because she's very young and she sees things as simply as a twelve or thirteen-year-old does. To her it's a baby, and she's fond of it regardless of who its father is. I think that makes me feel a certain hopefulness at the end.*

Stephanie: *There's something hopeful for me about the ending in that, after being killed by Voddiccia, Boadicea gets up and, as it were, looks at her dead body. There's a survival instinct within that.*

Performance Venues:

1995

15-17 June	Arts Centre	Warwick University
15-23 July	Fringe Festival	Winnipeg (Canada)
4-13 August	Fringe Festival	Saskatoon (Canada)
18-27 August	Fringe Festival	Edmonton (Canada)
1-8 September	Fringe Festival	Victoria (Canada)
9-17 September	Fringe Festival	Vancouver (Canada)
26/27 September	Theatr Gwynned	Bangor
28 September	Assembly Rooms	Ludlow
29/30 September	Midlands Arts Centre	Birmingham
2-4 October	Jackson's Lane	London
6 October	Buddle Arts Centre	Wallsend
7 October	Dovecot Arts Centre	Stockton-on-Tees
10 October	Arts Centre	Aberdeen
14 October	Harbour Arts Centre	Irvine, Strathclyde
20&21 October	Alhambra	Bradford
25-28 October	Komedia	Brighton
31 October	Arts Centre	Eastbourne
2 November	Arts Centre	Aberystwyth
3/4 November	Arena Theatre	Wolverhampton
7 November	Drama Dept.	Exeter University
8 November	Stertz Arts Centre	Cornwall
9 November	Arts Centre	Falmouth
11 November	Shrewsbury and District Arts Association	Shrewsbury
13 November	Peacock Theatre	Clifton
14 November	Corn Market Hall	Kettering
21 November	The Old Town Hall	Hemel Hempstead

Press Quotes

'Foursight Theatre Company resurrect another woman from the pages of history and bring her roaring into life again in their new production' (Ann Fitzgerald, *The Stage*, 20 July 1995)

'A triumph once more for this exceptionally talented group.' (Irene Tims, *Birmingham What's On*, September 1995)

'This British production is magnificent and it is mostly due to the exceptional and spirited performances by the cast of four ... Stand in line, it's worth it.' (Michele Le Tourneau, *Winnipeg Free Press*, 17 July 1995)

'a theatrical tour-de-force' (A.C. *Victoria Times*, 2 September 1995)

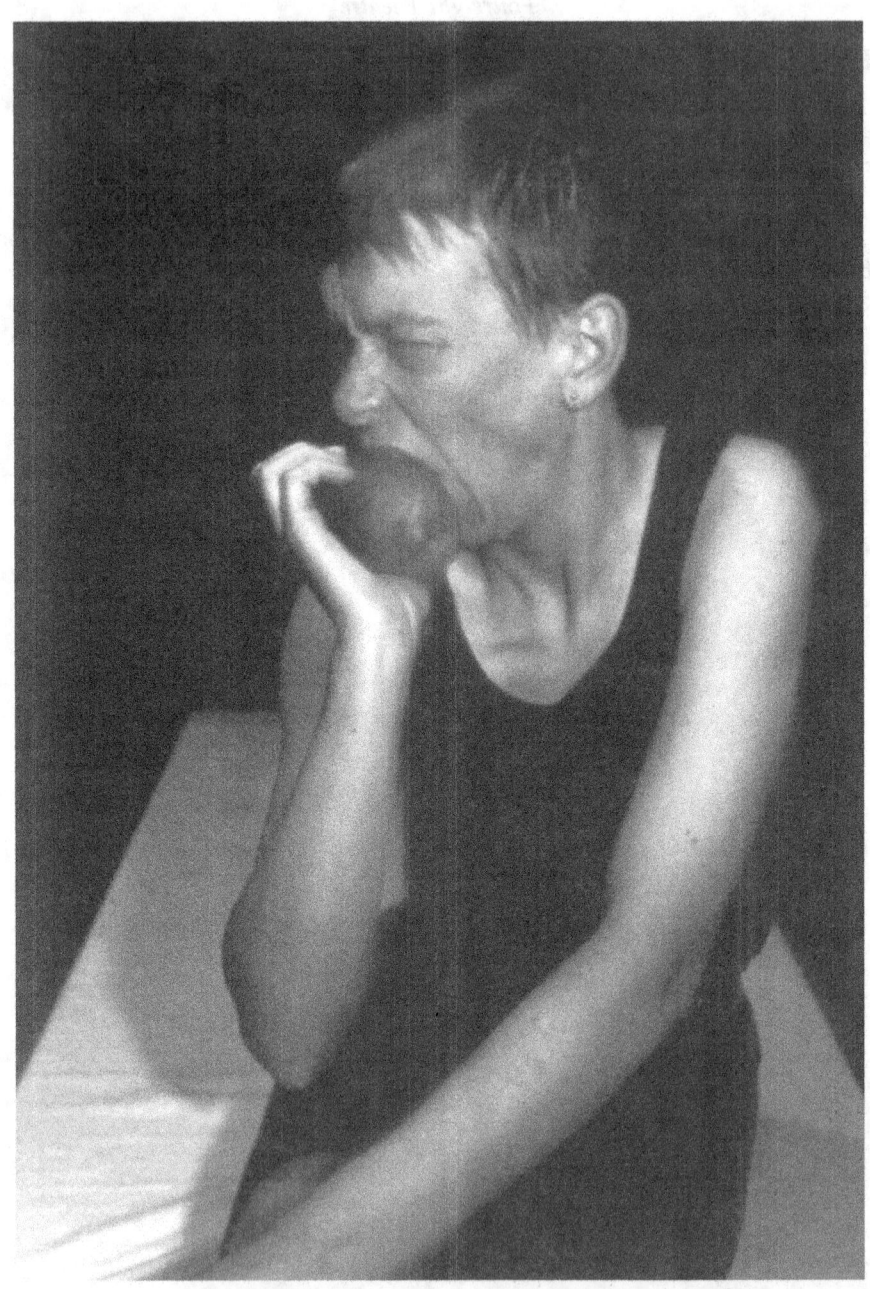

Slap, Foursight Theatre Company. Performer: Naomi Cooke. Photo: Gilbert Dong

Slap

Credits

Devised and written by   Naomi Cooke and Kate Hale
Performed by   Naomi Cooke
Directed by   Kate Hale

'We were ... interested in exploring virgin birthing' [Naomi Cooke, performer], 'exploring lesbian motherhood' [Kate Hale, director]

Slap in performance

A woman's voice speaks, slowly, out of the darkness. She's not afraid of the dark, she explains. 'It's a comfort', because in the dark it's possible to pretend that you're not there – until the 'vague memories catch up with you', that is, and then you begin to 'wonder where you went to' (*Slap*, unpublished script: 1).

There is a brief silence and then a match flares, fitfully illuminating a woman's (Gracie's) face, and her hands, which are engaged in lighting a lamp. Suddenly she freezes, listening intently. Was that a snore she heard? Her husband, Thomas O'Donnell, is recently dead and now she is afraid that he has come back to haunt her. Sitting in the warm, embracing dark of downstairs she feels safe, but the darkness upstairs is another matter. Upstairs is the site of her marriage bed, once the property of her dead husband – as she was his property when she was in it. Even now, Gracie can hear his breath in her ear, and she is assailed again by the terror that his lovemaking will result in her conceiving yet another child. When he was alive, she used to pray over and over to the Virgin Mary, always with the same intention: 'Holy Mother, please don't let me have another' (ibid.). Mary was, and still is, her chief solace because, even if the Father and the Son are busy doing other things, the Virgin Mary's always listening. 'She can see in the dark', too (ibid.), and she is therefore always there as a source of protection. Comforted and strengthened by this thought, Gracie douses the light in the lamp.

After a short blackout, the stage lights come up and Gracie is seen clearly for the first time. She has curly hair, wears a shiny red blouse, a dark skirt and elasticated pop socks which leave her knees bare. Her mood has changed with the altered lighting state and she is now both more confident and more lighthearted. As she folds a pile of sheets she talks to the audience, telling them first about her husband's foibles and then recreating for them – and for herself – the day of his funeral. In her mind's eye she sees the coffin being carried down the stairs, and the neighbours grouped outside the house. Above all, it is the faces of the women she remembers as they watched their men who, in their turn, were watching the coffin. '[T]ake it from me', Gracie says to the audience, 'there was some wishful thinking going on' (S.: 2). Her words are humorous and light, but they remind her of her earlier fears and she becomes more serious, imagining the women sitting, as she has sat, in the dark of their front rooms in the early hours of the morning, afraid to go to the beds that house their snoring husbands.

This evocation of a host of women, each one segregated in the darkness of a separate 'downstairs', returns Gracie to her nightmarish past of unwanted lovemaking and the horrors of repeated pregnancies. Her own hand becomes the hand of the importunate Thomas O'Donnell reaching out to grasp her breasts, while she struggles to push it away with her other hand. This frantic 'dance' of determined assault and attempted repulsion is accompanied by the strains of the 'Ave Maria' which gradually build in volume to fill the stage and auditorium with sound. The hand that represents Gracie's husband eventually succeeds in its quest and, as a result, she becomes convulsed by labour pains. Standing on the table, she screams first to her daughter (Shauna) to help her, then, as the pain escalates, to the Virgin Mary. Raising her arms in semblance of the crucified Christ, she pleads: 'Holy Mother let me die' (S.: 3). She continues however to inhabit the living world of pain and, crouched on the table, she mimes pulling out a baby from between her legs. Blood is draining away from her fast, and she wants to drain away with it. Once more she stands on the table, and, hugging to her chest (like a child's comfort blanket) a sheet that covers the table, she has a vision of herself with Mary – beyond pain and horror. Her 'dreams ha[ve] come true' (ibid.). Then the music of the 'Ave Maria' fades out and, in the ensuing silence, she remembers the sounds she heard at the time of the birth: bits of the dead baby dropping from her body into a bucket.

During the recreation of the birth of the dead baby the lights have dimmed. Now they brighten, and, once again matter of fact, Gracie kneels on the table and pulls towards herself a bag of potatoes. She spears one of the potatoes with a knife and begins to peel it, but it turns out to be bad – as her baby was. She's had seventeen babies, she tells the audience, four of whom died. In addition, there have been more miscarriages than she can remember. Her eldest child is Shauna and Shauna is her 'life's blood' (ibid.). She couldn't cope without her. It was Shauna who delivered the dead baby whose birth Gracie has just narrated. A 'brave girl' (ibid.), she never flinched once.

As she talks about her children, Gracie is occupied in preparing a meal – peeling potatoes and chopping liver. Then she begins to tidy the table, putting the peelings and bad bits of potato on to a newspaper to be thrown away. Like the potato and the dead baby, Gracie is now 'bad inside'. The doctors want to cut the 'bad' (S.: 4) out of her but Gracie can't see any point in this. After all, if they cut the 'bad' out, there won't be anything left. It's high time for her to be thrown away, she decides, along with the rubbish that she is putting on to the newspaper. This being the case, it is also high time for her to make a will, but, as she ruefully explains, it's difficult to know how to divide five hundred and fifty pounds between thirteen children, thirty-four grandchildren and five great grandchildren. As a possible aid to doing this sum, she picks up the chopping board with its mound of liver and begins to line up the pieces, so that each one represents a child. First there came Shauna, then, in the following order, Patrick, Sarah, Gerrard and John. Then she lost one – 'so that can go out with the rubbish' (ibid.: 5) – and Gracie throws the relevant piece of liver on to the newspaper with the bad bits of potato. Next came Moira and Caitlin, and then she lost another. A second piece of liver joins the discarded potato bits. Then came Luke, or, no, perhaps she's got the order wrong.

She begins to go through the names of her children once again from the beginning to make sure she's listing them correctly, and, as she does so, the sound of 'I Want to be an Old Woman' by Michelle Shocked fades in, and builds, so that it drowns out her voice. The lights dim and, in the semi-darkness, the performer playing Gracie unbuttons her red blouse. Turning her back to the audience, she begins the transformation into Shauna.

Shauna

When the lights come back up, Shauna is present. Her short hair is ornamented by a red headband, and she is dressed entirely in black - a long skirt, and a top with a design on the shoulders that is suggestive of epaulettes. Gracie has just died and Shauna is sorting out the house. She folds a pile of sheets, at the same time singing an Irish nationalist song. From time to time she breaks off and takes a swig from a bottle of whiskey. Having finished with the sheets, she puts the potatoes on to boil and tries, unsuccessfully, to peel the outer layer from an onion. She is unsuccessful because, as becomes increasingly obvious, she is both angry and distressed, and eventually, putting down the onion, she blurts out what is on her mind: 'How are you supposed to tell your own mother that she's given birth to a fucking mess?' (S.: 6). In the aftermath of Gracie's death, Shauna is reliving the brief entrance into the world all those years ago of the sibling who was born dead. On the table is a bowl of water, red from the liver Gracie washed in it, and Shauna picks up some potato peelings and drops them into the bloody water, saying as she does so, 'You wouldn't believe that something which smelt so bad could come out of something human' (ibid.).

As Gracie did before her, she narrates the story of the dead baby, this time from the perspective of a young girl staring between her 'mother's splayed legs wondering what would come out this time' (ibid.). Gracie had placed newspapers on the mattress to try to protect it, and, on the uppermost page, was a report about the shootings on 'Bloody Sunday': 'Thirteen Catholics slaughtered by the British Army for nothing more than asking them to leave' (ibid.). As Shauna's eyes fastened on the words, Gracie's blood seeped on to the newspaper so that it covered the picture of the killings: 'Blood blotting out blood' (ibid.).

For Shauna, this image became the catalyst which resulted, eventually, in her changing her life in three ways. She 'joined the IRA to stop the killings ... went on the pill ... to stop the birthings' (S.: 7) and got a divorce from the husband who disapproved of the latter action. The neighbourhood women disapproved too, and, at first, they would cross to the other side of the street to avoid her. When they were pregnant though it was a different story. Then they would come to Shauna asking for help. Their stupidity fills her with bitter rage. The pill is legal in Northern Ireland. The women could buy it two streets away, but they won't go against the Catholic Church's rules. 'Once the damage is done [though] they're quite prepared [to resort to] a hot bath and the knitting needle' (ibid.).

There is of course one way to avoid getting pregnant, Shauna sneers, and that is to 'Do it with women' (ibid.). There is a lengthy pause and then she quietly confides the fact that her daughter, Theresa, is a lesbian. To Shauna this is a slap in the face. She was determined that Theresa should know everything about sex, its pleasures as well as how to avoid conception, and Theresa's response has been to embrace a sexuality Shauna finds repugnant.

Her recounting of the birth of the dead baby, with its corollary of her conversion to the Republican cause, followed by her comments on heterosexual pleasure, lead Shauna into the narration of a story from her past in which death and sex are intermingled. It was night time, she recalls, and there was a riot in the distance. Then the feet of British soldiers could be heard, running down the street and, a few moments later, a voice in the next house: 'Where is he, you fucking taigs? We saw him come in here you lying bastards' (S.: 8). As she speaks the British soldier's words, Shauna faces upstage, her body and clenched fists evoking his aggressive stance. Then, she turns to face downstage, and, as a narrow beam of light traps her, she becomes the Republican soldier on the run from the British Army. His face is wet and he speaks fearfully, like a child. He's not crying, he claims, it's the gas stinging his eyes. Speaking again as herself, Shauna offers to get some vinegar to ease the pain. Her voice is gentle, lulling, suffused with a vulnerabilty and openness that match his. She holds her hands, palms up, in front of her in a way that is reminiscent of certain statues of the Virgin Mary, and her action evokes that of her mother (Gracie), standing on the table, arms lifted at her sides like Christ on the cross, begging Mary to let her die. Whereas Gracie pleaded for Mary's help in the bodily pose of her crucified son, however, Shauna casts herself as a sexualised version of Mary, at once maternal and sensually needy.

A few moments later, her hands once again recall – and reconfigure – Gracie's actions. Gracie used one of her hands to enact her husband's unwanted lovemaking, and now Shauna uses one of hers as that of the Republican soldier. In contrast to Gracie, repeatedly pushing away her husband's unwanted hand, Shauna uses her free hand to stroke the hand that represents the soldier's, tenderly cleaning a wound on it. Outside in the street there is the noise of bullets, inside, the touching of bodies - a way of fighting death. Shauna's narrative of her encounter with the soldier ends with the ringing of the 'phone. It was her mother, she recalls, checking whether she was all right. Yes, she reassured Gracie. She would 'be round soon'. 'Remember to close the back door as you leave', she said softly to the soldier (ibid.).

The lights fade and then come up again. The night of this lovemaking was also the night Theresa confided in her grandmother about her lesbianism, Shauna explains, though she didn't inform Shauna herself for another two years. Theresa had found it hard to tell her mother because Shauna 'didn't like women ... was forever blaming them' (ibid.). It's true, Shauna admits. She does prefer men. They make her feel sexy and strong. Perhaps that's wrong. Certainly she feels lonely now. She misses her mother, misses Theresa. As the lights dim, 'Irish Girls are Pretty' by The Proclaimers fades in and Shauna takes off her headband and skirt. Blackout.

Theresa

When the stage is once again illuminated, Theresa is revealed wearing a grey tank top and leggings cut off at the knee. Partially hidden beneath the tank top is a necklace of white beads. She is excited, first dancing to the music of The Proclaimers, then standing on the table to accompany them on an imaginary guitar. Jumping to the ground, she runs over to the stove, humming and moving to the music. There is the sound and smell of frying onions. As she stirs the cooking food, Theresa cheerfully informs the audience that, though a 'pregnant lesbian isn't everyone's idea of a good Catholic girl', nevertheless here she is, both a 'good Catholic and a pregnant lesbian' (S.: 9). She goes to mass, says her rosary (the 'necklace' of white beads), and she's both a virgin and an expectant mother – a reincarnation therefore of the Virgin Mary! 'St Peter will be tripping over himself to usher

[her] through the pearly gates. [She's] done it all – perhaps they'll make [her] a saint' (ibid.). She begins to dish up the food and, at the same time, like her mother and grandmother in their scenes, she becomes a storyteller. As Shauna did, she retells a tale her mother told, from her own perspective. Theresa's story, which is of the night of the riot, runs as follows.

She was sitting on the table at her grandmother's house, swinging her legs. Her uncle and aunt, aged three and four respectively, had their noses glued to the window with excitement, but at eighteen she was bored. She'd seen it all before. So had Gracie who was calmly stoking the fire as if nothing of note was happening. Without warning, Theresa found the words of a confession forming in her mouth. 'Gran', she said, 'I love women... like you love Grandad' (ibid.). For a longish time Gracie was silent, but at last she spoke: 'Well now, Theresa, you've found yourself a novel way of remaining a virgin, haven't you?' (ibid.). Her words made Theresa laugh at first, but, almost as quickly, she began to cry. She would have a hard life if she stayed in Northern Ireland, Gracie warned. She should get away while she was still young. Then, abruptly, Gracie changed the subject, telling Theresa to give her mother a ring to make sure she was all right.

When Shauna failed to answer the 'phone, Theresa was alarmed and she decided to go home to find out whether her mother was there. The riot had died down but the streets were full of soldiers, so she went the back way, thinking it would be safer. As Theresa recreates her night-time journey, the stage lights go out. She switches on a torch, directing it first towards the audience, and then using it to create sweeping arcs across the acting area. When her narrative reaches the point of her nervous approach to her mother's house, she turns partly upstage and holds the torch up to her face so that she is silhouetted in its beam. The house was in darkness when she reached it, she tells the audience, with the exception of a light in the pantry, against which two figures could be seen apparently struggling. She was about to call out, when she realised that they were not struggling, but making love – her 'mother and a man with a bleeding hand' (S.: 10). Stunned, she remained where she was, motionlessly watching her mother (here Theresa faces front and adjusts the torch so that it illuminates one side of her face) who was so powerful in her ability to love and fight men at the same time. Theresa stood there for a long time, overwhelmed by what she was witnessing. Then, the curtains were drawn at the window, and the lights went out. Quietly, she 'backed away' (ibid.), believing that she would never be able to tell her mother that she was interested neither in loving men nor fighting them. Shauna would think she was a coward.

Theresa switches off the torch and the lights come up. Her tone is once again bright, her movements lively. She did tell Shauna eventually, she explains, but only because Gracie left Theresa all her money when she died. Five hundred and fifty pounds: her 'ticket to freedom' (ibid.). No-one else got anything, so Theresa had to tell her mother then. Shauna didn't take it very well. She thought that Theresa had 'deserted Ireland', but, from Theresa's perspective, it's Ireland that's deserted her. She loves Ireland, but she had to choose 'which war [she] was going to fight' (ibid.) and it seemed to her that there was more hope for her cause than there was for that of Northern Ireland. Staying in Northern Ireland and living openly as a lesbian was anyway impossible. '[B]eing gay in Northern Ireland', she informs the audience, 'is like being a pig farmer at a Jewish wedding' (ibid.).

During the last few lines of dialogue Theresa has been sitting perched on the back of a wooden chair. Now, as she relives a visit to the 'one seedy gay bar in Belfast' (ibid.), she stands on the seat of the chair, her arms at her sides, as though she is being squeezed on all sides by the press of people, and a tight shaft of light holds her captive in that position. Everyone in the room was nervous, she explains, because of the effort of getting there without being seen, and there was always a question you had to ask before getting to know anyone: 'Which school did you go to?' (ibid.). If the answer had a saint in the title you knew you were all right because you were with a Catholic. On this particular night though she didn't need to ask because, there, in the corner, drinking a half pint of Guinness, was an old classmate, Lizbeth O'Leary, the beautiful Lizbeth O'Leary who used to be her partner when they did country dancing. Once, after country dancing, Theresa and Lizbeth carried the record player back to the resources cupboard together, and, in its accommodating darkness, they exchanged a kiss. Theresa was so overwhelmed that she wasn't sure whether to be sick or take all her clothes off and dance 'a jig for joy'(S.: 11).

Theresa's response to the perturbation the kiss caused her was to repeat over and over the words of the 'Hail Mary', in an attempt to make her feelings for Lizbeth go away. Instead, however, the prayer had the effect of reassuring her about the rightness of her feelings. She recalls a momentary vision she had of Mary, and this evokes her grandmother's experience in the first scene, but, whereas for Gracie the Holy Mother was a solace in the midst of agony and horror, for Theresa she acted as a passport to an exploration of the person she most deeply knew herself to be. Mary didn't condemn her. She smiled because she knew that Theresa was in love and that she wasn't 'harming anyone' (ibid.).

And, suddenly, two years later, Lizbeth was again in the same room as Theresa. To calm her nerves, Theresa began to count to ten, but only managed to get as far as three before she made 'her move'. 'I know this isn't country dancing', she said to Lizbeth O'Leary', 'but how do you fancy a polka?' (ibid.). It was, she reminisces, the best night of her life. Eighteen months later they left Northern Ireland together, but they never left the club together. 'A secret is a precious thing in Northern Ireland' (ibid.).

Theresa jumps down from the chair and the lights come up to illuminate the whole of the acting area. She and Lizbeth have only had one real row in the time they've been together, she tells the audience, and that was at the fertility clinic. Two Irish Catholics, they were both so nervous about what they were doing that they were terrified to make the final decision, and, instead, they began to argue about the kind of donor they wanted. Eventually, Theresa stuck a pin in a name and they made the decision that way. It's an excellent method of having a baby, she suggests. After all, there's no danger 'of the father running off and leaving you in the lurch' (ibid.), is there? Admittedly some people think it's unnatural, but 'what does natural mean? If it means having seventeen babies [like Gracie] ... and then dying in agony, never even having had an orgasm, then [Theresa's] way over there in loony land' (ibid.).

She moves over to the table and lies back on it, wondering, as she does so, how she is going to tell her mother that she's pregnant. She has thought of 'phoning, but Shauna is always busy with one campaign or another. So it's probably best to write a letter instead. 'Dear Ma', she begins. She thinks for a moment, and then continues:

> I hope you're keeping well. I heard about the bomb blast in Belfast last week. I 'phoned our Jamie and he said you were all OK. So thank God for that. My prayers must be getting through. I've got some news to tell you. I think it's really good news and I hope you will too. I'm having a baby! (ibid.)

The last sentence is blurted out in a tone of amazement and great joy, but then Theresa is humorously appalled at Shauna's likely response. To the sound of Paul Anka's '(You're) Having My Baby' she begins the letter once again. The lights fade to black, and, at the same time, the music changes to 'Che Sera, Sera' – what will be, will be!

Naomi Cooke (performer) and and Kate Hale (director) on the creation and reception of Slap

(Naomi was a founding member of Foursight Theatre. In 1992 she left the company for a time and went to work in Canada. *Slap* was her first project with Foursight after this interim period.)

***Finding a basic structure – Kate**: One of the last shows Naomi did with Foursight before she went to Canada was a one-woman piece,* Pink Smoke in the Vatican, *which I directed. We both loved working on that project and we felt that the end result really hit what we were trying to achieve, both stylistically and contentwise. In 1994 I had a sabbatical from Foursight and I decided to go over to Canada and work with Naomi again. We were trying to be aware of what had worked well in* Pink Smoke *but, at the same time, we wanted to find a different dynamic.*

Naomi: *At the beginning we were thinking of doing a two-hander because we had already worked on a one-woman show and we wanted to do something new and challenging.*

Kate: *We decided to employ a man as the second performer because Naomi was very interested in working with a kind of energy that hadn't been available in the work she'd previously done with Foursight. Also, because initially we were working outside the remit of Foursight, we felt at liberty to do something other than biographical theatre.*

Naomi: *The original plan was to do a play about genetic engineering, and we were also interested in exploring the concept of virgin birthing. That's where the link with* Slap, *as it eventually evolved, comes in.*

Kate: *For Naomi and myself as individuals motherhood was also becoming a question. We were approaching our thirties, and we were beginning to wonder whether we wanted to have children. We were also interested in exploring lesbian motherhood. The genetic engineering idea was one Foursight had worked on in* Frankenstein's Mothers, *but neither Naomi nor I had been involved in that project, and we wanted to see where our ideas led to.*

Naomi: *What we eventually came up with was a massage-parlour setting as a basis for the action. The male performer, who by this time we'd found, would be the masseur and I would be the person going for a massage. At that point the style of the piece derived from the slap of the masseur, and the intention was that he would draw stories out of my body.*

Kate: *Stories of different mothers coming out of one woman's body. Massaging an arm would release the arm story, for example, and massaging the buttock would release the buttock story. We were trying to express various aspects of motherhood, including lesbian motherhood and virgin motherhood. One story was of a perpetual mother, dropping babies right left and centre, and this eventually led to Gracie, who is the first character in* Slap *as it is now.*

Unfortunately, as we worked on the massage-parlour idea, we gradually realised that our concept of physical theatre and image work was very different from that of the male performer we were employing. We hadn't been able to workshop him in a proper way, and, with hindsight, it was foolish to employ someone without that.

Naomi: *Eventually he dropped out and we were faced with the question of what we were going to do. We'd got five weeks left and then we had to open with a show called* Slap. *So we said to each other, "What's really gripped us?", and the answer was the virgin mother, and the Catholic setting, which was very rich and dense.*

Kate: *What chiefly inspired us were two books:* Only the Rivers Run Free *(subtitled* Northern Ireland: The Women's War*), based on interviews with Catholic and Protestant women, and a radical text on the virgin mother,* Born of a Woman *by John Shelby Spong.*

Naomi: *He argues that the physical fact of the virgin birth isn't true, though an inner truth and understanding remain.*

Kate: *He also writes about sexuality in a very radical way. So we thought, "How can we contextualise these two books?" One end of the spectrum for us was Gracie, living by the Catholic creed, and basically killing herself with birthing. The other was the thing that is spearheading the women's movement now: the concept of lesbian birth. Consequently, we had two polar positions from which to explore the development of women's relationship to motherhood. On the one hand, it's been seen by feminists as something that traps women; on the other, it's our power base, and the question arises: 'Who is it denied to?'. This raises issues of abortion, the rights of women against motherhood, and within motherhood, etc.*

The reason for the Catholic setting was that it enabled us to make a direct comparison between virgin birth and lesbian ideas of birth we wanted to explore. While we were in Canada we talked to a Northern Irish lesbian who told us that in Northern Ireland the two extremes we were looking at do co-exist. Catholicism continues to exert a stranglehold on so many people because of the desire to remain committed to one political aim – the unification of Ireland – and the sense that to go against Catholicism is to go against that aim. The pressure pushes people to the limit, and there's a very strict understanding of ways of behaving. So, whereas in our society it's unusual to find a character like Gracie, in Northern Ireland Gracies are still very much part of the fabric of society.

For a long time we worked with just two characters, Gracie and a modern-day character, but eventually this began to feel clichéd.

Naomi: *We were asking too much. Going from the first of these characters to the second was too stark. Then we realised that what we actually had was a grandmother and a granddaughter, and what we needed was the mother. So, in came Shauna.*

Kate: *For me she's like the confusion of feminism.*

Naomi: *1970s, loving men and hating them. She's very complex. A lot of aspects of her character came from* Only the Rivers Run Free. *I remember the most stirring story for me from the book (in relation to Shauna) was that of a woman talking about making love while the bombs were going off, and what a life source that was for her – forming the creative potential of humankind when there is so much destruction going on.*

Kate: *In many ways Shauna developed thematically and structurally rather than characterwise, in that our need for her was thematic and structural rather than arising from a sense that we needed another character. We needed a contrast from both Gracie and the modern-day figure who rejects everything that Granny stood for.*

Naomi: *Except that she doesn't!*

Kate: *Exactly! Shauna gave us space, through what she rejects, and accepts from her background, to move to what the modern-day figure (Theresa) rejects and accepts in her turn – from her grandmother and her mother. There was a greater richness in the positioning of three characters than there had been in the comparison between only two. Shauna constituted a reality that threw up further questions regarding the positions of the other two characters. She was everything for me that made you think again. You can't pigeon-hole women, or feminists, or women's theatre. It released us from feeling that we were on a track about how badly women are treated and oppressed. Shauna was so dynamic and active, as well as bitter, and resentful, and negative in many ways. Her reactions were quite different from those of her mother and daughter, and this gave us a much clearer sense of how we affect each other as women, rather than the piece becoming women versus patriarchy.*

I think Foursight has always been very interested in looking at how women relate to each other, the intricacies of women's sociological and psychological make-up within patriarchy, but without continually making it into a blame situation, a struggle situation. Women make certain choices within a patriarchal framework, which lead in a variety of directions, some of which result in a questioning of the society we live in, others in an acceptance of it. Gracie and Shauna present two sets of responses, then, in Theresa, you have someone making compromises. The rejection that we were able to put into Shauna enabled the third character to be post rejection. Without that central character the modern-day character would have had to reject everything to get a polemic going.

The devising and writing process – Naomi: *The work process was very dramatic because the play seemed to birth itself. It was as though it had been sitting inside us both. We did a lot of studio work: improvising, setting up situations and drawing narratives out of them. Then we'd go home, sit down with what we'd got and play with it.*

Kate: *Because we know each other so well it was a completely different scenario from* Boadicea. *You could just be comfortable and brave enough to say sometimes that what we'd worked on that day wasn't good, and we were going in the wrong direction. By going in the wrong direction however we could see what direction we* **did** *need to go in, so the practical work always facilitated the writing, whether we wrote up the improvisation or wrote cold. Sometimes Naomi would be at the* typewriter and I would walk round the room shouting out lines. We'd choose which ones to use later.

Naomi: In the rehearsal room we'd work with what we'd got, sometimes reimprovising it. It was a very simple process. A lot of it was based in the body – drawing stories out of the body.

Kate: Yes. We kept the idea of releasing stories from the body. We also did a lot of work on the chakras, based on the different emotions the various chakras have attached to them. With Gracie it was the neck chakra, which is to do with memory.

Naomi: One day Kate told me she wanted me just to massage my neck and see what happened. It's quite amazing what does happen when you massage your neck.

Kate: You have to go really deeply into it because the neck is a very vulnerable area. That power of being vulnerable is at the root of the sort of theatre I want to create.

Naomi: Integrity and vulnerability. If you see dishonest theatre that isn't vulnerable, it's dead.

The interpersonal dynamic of the work process – Naomi: The fact that I'm a committed Christian and Kate's a committed atheist also fed the work in terms of the way we approached it, and what it means to us. Although I find much of the church doctrine embedded in Catholicism hard to embrace, ultimately I share in the same Christian faith. I'm a Protestant by denomination, and getting in touch with these Catholic women's faiths, and trying to communicate something of that, was important to me. I believe there is a real truth there, and it's rarely explored in the medium of theatre.

Kate: For me Catholicism has far more impact as a social force than other branches of Christianity. It's more controlling, and, as a political being, that's what I'm interested in. As a woman I find its political power even more significant. For me it's part of the world I live in, and I don't think religion belongs to anyone in particular because it affects and pressurises the social rules that we all live under. I also think the power that is given to the Virgin Mary is central to how Christianity in the past has led to the place where we are now as women. So that for me is intellectually and politically interesting. I've become far more liberal than I used to be towards religion as a concept because at least it opens you to the fact that, within these constraints, people are thinking, and they're not being brainwashed. In a way that's what the play deals with as well: how much the structure is a restrictive thing, and how much it's a basis from which to explore ideas.

Naomi: *I also think that the fact that Kate's straight and I'm gay is very important. My personal journey created a kind of dynamic that we were able to feed into this piece because the modern-day character, who one expects is going to reject the faith (like her mother), in fact embraces it, while living a life that the faith utterly rejects.*

Performing a one-woman show – Naomi: *Prior to* Slap, *I'd just done a two-person show again after performing one-woman pieces for a while, and I realised how different the dynamic is when you're on stage with somebody else. I really rather like being on stage by myself, and I'm not exactly sure what that's about. Partly, it's because I thoroughly enjoy the dynamic between the performer and the audience. It's heightened I think when you're on your own because you're not relating to another performer and learning their rhythms, and patterns, and pulls. The one-performer/audience dialogue has been a very enjoyable experience for me. It's so direct and vulnerable, and, again, honesty has to be the heart of it.*

Kate: *I think the directness is exciting. Also, it's usually storytelling-based work, which is so powerful, and I think that theatre has lost a sense of that. It's having a renaissance, but it's very much associated with children. Look at Alan Bennett's* Talking Heads *and the power that has. I find it ludicrous that television doesn't use these techniques more, and, when it happens in theatre – with a Shakespeare soliloquy, for example, or in a modern piece – it's so lovely because you're being acknowledged as an audience. It heightens the idea of what theatre's about, which is communication between people on stage and the audience.*

Costume - Kate: *We talked at great length about all of the costumes, practically and thematically. With Shauna we were interested in the scandalousness of being glamorous in the wrong situations, like secretaries at school who dress up to the nines. It seems inappropriate. For Shauna it was the inappropriateness of being glamorous and sophisticated in the Falls Road. We wanted someone who was involved and affected by what was going on, but it's like putting on a layer. Again, the very long clean look of Shauna's costume derived from the idea of her wanting to surpass her situation and be something other.*

Naomi: *I think there's also a clear statement in it of her as a sexual being.*

Kate: *Gracie's shiny red top was for me the part of her personality that is conveyed by all her little comic interjections. It reveals the fact that she's not quite going under. Perhaps she was out shopping one day, and was about to buy a grey cardigan, and then she saw the red top, and she thought she'd have that bit of jolly instead. It's like a refusal to give up hope. It's also an incongruousness which I think rounds off her character.*

Food – Kate: *The liver that Gracie chops up is very much associated with her character. Foursight has a tradition of using food in shows, and I think we're always looking for food imagery. One of the improvisations we used in rehearsal was based on what sort of colour, food, etc the character would be, and Naomi realised that Gracie would be liver and onions. So that's how the liver came into the show, and, once the structure began to fall into place, through finding the Shauna character, the preparation and cooking of the food became very important. We worked on the improvisation of Naomi chopping the liver, and counting out the children so that the ones she'd lost went out with the rubbish, quite early on. This led to the idea of the birth of the baby – the bits dropping into the bucket, and the potatoes dropping in the water. There are also Gracie's words about there being more blood in the liver than there is in her. It's the idea of life-blood, and also Christ's blood. In the context of what we were looking at that particular food had a very rich, symbolic journey to go on – the preparing and cooking and eating.*

The other thing about the liver which was important to me is my memory that my grandmother told me that, when women were anaemic in pregnancy, they had to eat raw liver because there weren't iron tablets then. That always struck me as an image from childhood. Eating raw liver made the pregnant woman in my mind into a sort of monster.

Audience responses – Naomi: *I've had several conversations with people from Northern Ireland who are now living in Canada and the responses were very positive. They all felt it was true to the reality of the situation. When we were devising the show we spoke specially with two lesbian Northern-Irish women, one Protestant and one Catholic, and some of their experiences made their way into the piece.*

Kate: *Naomi and I had a conversation with one woman who objected to the idea that we were telling Irish women's stories when we'd never been to Belfast. I pointed out that it's something I really care about and have my own feelings around, and was very much inspired to do. Afterwards, I felt guilty for a while. I panicked because I wondered if she had a point. Thinking about it further, though, it's like a man doing a piece about women – which happens anyway all the time. My argument would be that there's room for both. There's room for people it directly affects and room for people who are coming in and studying it from the outside, bringing their own issues to it.*

Performance venues:

1996

9-10 February	Arts Centre	Warwick University
17 February	Theatre in the Mill	Bradford University
23 February	The Live Theatre	Newcastle upon Tyne
27 February-2 March	Jackson's Lane	London
6 March	Oakengates Theatre	Telford
7 March	Taleisen Arts Centre	Swansea
8 March	Guildhall Arts Centre	Gloucester
9 March	Arena Theatre	Wolverhampton
20 March	William Brookes School	Much Wenlock
21 March	Midlands Arts Centre	Birmingham
31 October	Arts Centre	Eastbourne
2 November	Arts Centre	Aberystwyth
3&4 November	Arena Theatre	Wolverhampton
7 November	Drama Dept.	Exeter University
8 November	Arts Centre	St Austell
9 November	Arts Centre	Falmouth
11 November	The Gateway	Shrewsbury
13 November	Peacock Theatre	Clifton
14 November	Corn Market Hall	Kettering
21 November	The Old Town Hall	Hemel Hempstead

Slap was also performed in Canada in 1994 and 1995. The following quotations from reviews and CBC radio refer to Canadian performances.

Press Quotes

'This is a gritty, visceral drama. It has the stinging impact of a slap'. (Sheila Robertson, *The Star Phoenix* (Saskatoon), 3 August 1994)

'spendidly acted and intelligently written. It's raw, powerful life-affirming theatre'. (Adrian Chamberlain, *Times Colonist*, 4 February 1995)

'the fearless performance by Naomi Cooke ... leaves one breathless'. (C T, *The Georgia Straight*, 3-10 February 1995)

'One of the most brilliant actors I've ever seen. She portrays three generations of an Irish family and it is an absolute joy to watch ... A wonderful play.' (CBC Radio)

3

THE SPHINX THEATRE COMPANY

Productions Prior to *Voyage in the Dark* and *Goliath*

1973	– *Instrument for Love* by Jennifer Phillips
1973	– *The Amiable Courtship* of Miz Venus and Wild Bill by Pam Gems
1973	– *Lovefood* by Dinah Brook
1973	– *Mal de Mere* by Micheline Wandor
1973	– *Parade of Cats* by Jane Wibberly
1974	– *Fantasia* by the company
1975/6	– *My Mother Says I Never Should* by the company
1976/7	– *Work to Role* by the company
1977	– *Out on the Costa Del Trico* by the company
1977/8	– *Pretty Ugly* by the company
1978	– *In Our Way* by the company
1978/9	– *Hot Spot* by Eileen Fairweather and Melissa Murray
1979	– *Soap Opera* by Donna Franceschild
1979/80	– *The Wild Bunch* by Bryony Lavery
1980	– *My Mkinga* by the company
1980/1	– *Better a Live Pompey than a Dead Cyril* by Claire McIntyre and Stephanie Nunn
1980/1	– *Breaking Through* by Timberlake Wertenbaker
1981	– *New Anatomies* by Timberlake Wertenbaker
1982	– *Time Pieces* by Lou Wakefield and the company
1982	– *Double Vision* by Libby Mason
1983	– *Love and Dissent* by Elisabeth Bond
1983	– *Dear Girl* by Libby Mason and Tierl Thompson
1984	– *Trade Secrets* by Jacqui Shapiro
1984/5	– *Pax* by Deborah Levy
1985	– *Anywhere to Anywhere* by Joyce Halliday
1985	– *Witchcraze* by Bryony Lavery
1986	– *Fixed Deal* by Paulette Randall
1986	– *Our Lady* by Deborah Levy
1987	– *Holding the Reins* by the company
1987	– *Lear's Daughters* by the company, with Elaine Feinstein
1988	– *Picture Palace* by Winsome Pinnock
1988	– *Lear's Daughters* by the company, with Elaine Feinstein
1989	– *Pinchdice & Co.* by Julie Wilkinson
1989	– *Zerri's Choice* by Sandra Yaw

1990   – *Mortal* by Marco Green and Caroline Griffin
1990   – *Her Aching Heart* by Byrony Lavery
1990   – *Christmas Without Herods* by Lisa Evans
1991   – *Her Aching Heart* by Bryony Lavery
1992   – *The Roaring Girl's Hamlet* by William Shakespeare, in a setting by Claire Luckham
1992/3   – *Every Bit Of It* by Jackie Kay
1993   – *Playhouse Creatures* by April De Angelis
1994   – *Chandralekha* by Amrit Wilson
1994   – *Black Sail White Sail* by Hélène Cixous
1995   – *Hanjo* by Seami, adapted by Diane Esguerra & by Yukio Mishima, translated by Donald Keene

Glass Ceilings (women's theatre conferences)

Shortly after taking over as Artistic Director of the Women's Theatre Group (soon to be renamed the Sphinx) Sue Parrish organised a women's theatre conference at the Institute of Contemporary Arts in London. Entitled 'The Glass Ceiling', this conference took place on 2 November 1991. It has been followed by similar events in subsequent years. Details of venues and major contributors are given below.

1991 at the ICA

Professor Janet Todd, Dr Juliet Dusinberre (Chaired by Sue Parrish)
Janet Todd, Fiona Shaw, Charlotte Keatley, Jill Tweedie (Chaired by Jenni Murray)

1992 at the ICA

Hélène Cixous, Sarah Cornell (Chaired by Sue Parrish)
Hélène Cixous, Janet Suzman, Deborah Warner, Fiona Shaw, Jackie Kay (Chaired by Jenni Murray)

1993 at the Royal National Theatre

Beatrix Campbell, Suzy Orbach (Chaired by Sue Parrish)
Hélène Cixous, Viv Gardner, Juliet Stevenson, Di Trevis, Rona Munro (Chaired by Jude Kelly)

1994 at the RNT

Taslima Nasrin, Irina Ratushinskaya, Amrit Wilson (Chaired by Helena Kennedy QC.)
Jude Kelly, Beatrix Campbell, Phyllis Nagy, Judith Jacob (Chaired by Ruth Mackenzie)

1995 at the RNT

Della Grace, Professor Susan Bassnett, (Chaired by Sarah Dunant)
Claire Armitstead, Annie Castledine, Kay Mellor, Toyah Willcox, Denise Wong (Chaired by Ruth Mackenzie)

1996 at the RNT

Dr Germaine Greer and Dr Juliet Mitchell
A reading of Sarah Kane's *Blasted*
Annie Castledine, Pam Gems, Bonnie Greer, Sarah Kane, Mel Kenyon (Chaired by Jude Kelly)

Sue Parrish: Artistic Director of Sphinx Theatre Company

The beginning: From 1971, there had been a loose, ad-hoc women's street theatre group, known as The Punch and Judies, who performed political devised pieces at demonstrations and similar events. Their work included a touring show in 1972 called The Amazing Equal Pay Play, *which concerned Barbara Castle and the Equal Pay Act and centred around a debate between a Labour and a Conservative M.P..*

After that early company disbanded, a group was set up in 1973 to read and discuss the work of women playwrights, in preparation for a Women's Festival inspired by Ed Berman of the Almost Free Theatre on Leicester Square. Meetings took the form of 'open sessions' and were attended by mainstream professionals, fringe practitioners, and people altogether new to the theatre. After the success of the Women's Festival, which focused on the work of women playwrights, women directors and women stage management, two companies were set up: The Women's Theatre Group and the short-lived Women's Company.

The Women's Theatre Group, as Sphinx was originally known, was started in 1973 by a group of actresses who had worked mainly with political theatre groups such as Belt and Braces, Red Ladder and 7:84. It was the first all-women group, though there have been many such groups since, all mining different aspects of feminism and performance. The first shows by The Women's Theatre Group were devised pieces about equal rights. From these, they moved on to inviting writers to create plays on specific issues. A number of well-known women dramatists – Timberlake Wertenbaker, for example, Clare McIntyre, Winsome Pinnock – have seen their first shows performed with The Women's Theatre Group.

When I joined the company in 1990 it was at a critical point of change. Financially it was in deficit, and audiences had been falling off. A properly researched project was in operation, the aim of which was to find out how the company was perceived. Letters were sent to people on our mailing list, and to critics and actors. Questionnaires were handed out to audiences at other companies' shows, and from all this information we were able to see that the company was still regarded as an agit-prop, political, seventies-style group, even though this no longer reflected the nature of the work that was being produced. For whatever combination of reasons, the old-style political audience has disappeared, and, though the company's work already reflected this change, it wasn't generally perceived. So it was crucial to reinforce the new identity that had developed. Renaming the company was part of this process.

The woman writer and the importance of form: *By 1990, the company was already very much focused on the woman writer, and I've worked to strengthen that. I believe that it's very important that women have the space and freedom to realise themselves as artists. 'Artist' is a somewhat unfashionable word today (unless it's used to refer to a visual artist). If it is used in the context of a writer, that writer is usually male. I think it's important to think of the woman writer as an artist in order to give her the opportunity to recognise herself as a subject in her own right, so that she can create roles for actresses of female characters who are themselves subjects in their own right. A visitor from Mars looking at film or television, or even many plays, today would conclude that women were creatures with reproductive and decorative functions, and sometimes supportive, hand-holding functions, but hardly that they were protagonists in their own story. Even when they're antagonists, they usually conform to some convenient stereotype, such as virago or harridan.*

The need to free women as subjects also relates to form. It seems to me essential to get away from present-day forms of naturalism and realism because the minute you start describing, in any kind of detail, modern women's lives you lock them into a psychic past which is to do with being a handmaid – a wife, mother, sister, tart or whatever.

Sphinx Theatre Company's production of *Voyage in the Dark* by Jean Rhys, adapted by Joan Wiles, first performed at the Young Vic Studio in 1996. Performers: (left to right) Ian Kirkby, Katrina Syran and Michael Vaughan. Directed by Sue Parrish. Designer: Franziska Wilcken. Music: Claire van Kampen. Choreographer: Claire Russ. Lighting designer: Jenny Kagan. Photo: Dee Conway

Voyage in the Dark

by Jean Rhys
adapted for the stage by Joan Wiles

Credits

Ethel, Maudie, Francine, Landlady	Hazel Holder
Vincent, Uncle Bo, Walter, Doctor, Preacher, Carl	Ian Kirkby
Anna	Katrina Syran
Walter, Joe	Michael Vaughan
Laurie, Germaine, Hester, Landlady, the Abortionist	Anne White
Director	Sue Parrish
Music by	Claire van Kampen
Designer	Franziska Wilcken
Lighting	Jenny Kagan
Choreographer	Claire Russ
Dance Teacher	Wendy Allnutt
Dialect Coach	Julia Wilson-Dixon
Production Manager	Petrus Bertschinger
Technical Manager	Andy Shewan
Stage Manager	Jane McKeown
Set Construction	Robert Batchelor
Furniture made by	Rolf Driver and Vikki Heron
Set painted by	Tim Davies
Costumes	David Plunkett
Production Photography	Dee Conway
Press	Chapman Duncan Assoc.
General Manager	Janet Waugh
Administrator	Alison Gagen

Sue Parrish, director of Voyage in the Dark

The 'woman as victim' myth: *My brief as Artistic Director of the Sphinx is to stage dramatic writing by women, either original plays or adaptations. As well as being written by a female dramatist the work must take women forward in some way. So it's my job to arbitrate what that new ground is. Currently, I'm interested, along with a good number of other feminists, in exploring what feminity is. Specifically, I'm concerned with trying to assess the legacy of the 'woman as victim' myth, because, until we can disinter this, and other related myths, and replay them in order to re-evaluate them, we can't be free of them.*

Perceptions of what a victim is are anyway not simple. On the one hand there is the fact that women have been trained to think of themselves as victims, and that our culture continues to exploit this – to re present it. On the other hand, women **are** *at the sticky end of patriarchal culture. They have been, and often still are, victims. Apart from anything else, they lack the economic power and physical strength of men. What is vital, though, is to separate out reality and myth.*

Hanjo: *My project prior to* Voyage in the Dark, Hanjo *was an exploration of a 'woman as victim'. It consisted of two related plays: an English adaptation of a fourteenth-century Japanese Noh play, and an updating of the same play by Yukio Mishima. The original version depicts the story of a prostitute who falls in love with a man with whom she has spent one night of love before he has to go off on a pilgrimage. The play has a happy ending because the lover comes and finds her.*

In Mishima's version, however, the setting is transformed to the 1950s, and a woman painter rescues the first woman (the prostitute), and takes her to Tokyo, where, every day, the woman dresses up in her best and goes to the station in the hope that her lover will come and find her. The newspapers get hold of her story, and eventually the lover does turn up, at the painter's house. The painter may, or may not, be lesbian, but that isn't really the point. What Mishima depicts is one woman who is possessed by a romantic myth, and another, the painter, who, through looking after the woman, is living vicariously off the same myth.

What actually happens, though, when the woman meets her lover, is that she doesn't recognise him, and she sends him away. The painter then sees her romantic myth crumble because she realises that the other woman is mad and that for the rest of her life she will be caring for a madwoman. It's a cruel inversion of the original story, but very modern. It throws up questions about the way in which we invest in romance. Women (heterosexual women at least) still have to negotiate a life with men, and romance is part of that. I felt that it was very valuable to step outside our own culture and look at a very heightened, ritualistic, formal culture where the issues and ideas could be seen more clearly.

It was a production that elicited very divergent responses. Some people loved it, and others thought it was reactionary. There's also the complexity that the woman's reaction in not recognising her lover may not be a symptom of madness. One could argue that she has found her own space within a romantic myth. As is the way with Japanese art, it's very subtle and multi-layered, but that was part of the exploration of romantic myth that I was engaged in. It was a very undogmatic exploration because I think dogma has passed its sell-by date.

Voyage in the Dark *is a further exploration of the 'woman as victim' myth. Jean Rhys is usually seen as a creator of passive heroines – women victims – but that's not the way I see her. It's true that, if you concentrate on the narrative line in* Voyage in the Dark, *Anna, the protagonist, sounds like a victim: innocent girl arrives from somewhere else (virtually from another planet, as it seems to her), and falls victim to the social codes and corrupt mores of this country. In particular,* she's a victim of the way upper-class men have divided their sexuality from their emotions, and, having no means of supporting herself, she then becomes further victimised through her role as, what would be termed in today's parlance, a sex worker. That's the narrative line. However I think the way Jean Rhys contextualises Anna's journey complicates the notion of her as a victim.

Black and white relationships: *One very important aspect of* Voyage in the Dark *is the way in which Jean Rhys brings into the light the nightmare of the poisoning of relationships between black and white in the West Indies. Colonialism and slavery are part of our history – as Britons and Europeans – that is still not talked about. There are huge psychic complexities that need to be resolved. In Rhys's work the sense of chaos and loss and bitterness are there with absolute clarity. When we started working on the book we all jumped and shuddered every time anybody said the word 'nigger'. It's a taboo word, and quite rightly of course. But it's got to be looked at and faced, and none of the critics have really done that. The reviews have concentrated on what I would call the 'dressing up' of the production. They've been very flattering about that, but they haven't looked at the meat of what Anna says about black being warm and gay, and white being cold and hard. Of course this may all be simply inside Anna's head, but it is her true experience and it needs to be looked at.*

For Anna in the novel, and also for Jean Rhys herself, the West Indies represents a place where everything is perfection, but the paradise also has a dark side because of the poisoned relationships I have mentioned. Francine was Anna's best friend, as well as the servant who attended her, and the person she relied upon, but Francine also hated her because she was part of the master race. So, on a personal level, history has intervened to poison relationships between the children. I don't think this is fully resolved in the novel, but I hope in our dramatization it's uncomfortable enough for people to meditate upon, even if only on a subconscious level.

Time: *Another important thing about Jean Rhys's work is the way she moves backwards and forwards in time, sometimes changing tense in the middle of a sentence. In* Voyage in the Dark *she moves from the past, when Anna was perhaps fifteen, or ten, to the time when she's writing the book and is apparently much older, and also to the present tense of the book's events. When I first read* Voyage in the Dark *I was reminded of T.S. Eliot, especially* The Waste Land, *and of course Jean Rhys was writing at the same time as Eliot, when artists were clearly experiencing a level of consciousness of time that was the result of pre, and post, First-World-War Modernism. Rhys's work is much closer to the poets of her time than it is, say, to the great narrative novelists of the nineteenth century, and, for me, that chimed with a very modern sensibility. 'Time' is one of the pressures on anyone alive today: the sense that history has stopped in some ways, that time is finite, and that probably life stops at death. These are very twentieth-century concerns, and they're very much part of* Voyage in the Dark.

The book is set in 1912, but Rhys wrote it in the early 1930s. Though it's built around autobiographical remembrances, it's clearly not specific to 1912. There are no distinct references to what people would have been wearing or doing, no horse-drawn cabs, or stays, for example, or any of the things that would mark the time as 1912. The book has the flavour of the thirties, and it seemed to me appropriate to bring the time forward in the production to the early 1940s, because there's something about the social collapse which happened around the Second World War, and which happens in film noir, that I think the story slightly prefigures.

Time is also important in the book because of Rhys's focus on the fleetingness of meeting and parting – the way people come together for a time and then part. This was one of the reasons why I chose to use the image of the tango in the production – because of the way it captures this fleetingness. It captures too the sense of twentieth-century alienation and rootlessness that is such a crucial part of the book. The choreographer and I were lucky enough to see the show, **Forever Tango,** *at the Strand Theatre (London) last summer, and that confirmed our view that the tango was the right metaphor for the production.*

A metaphorical structure was important because I wanted to tell the story in a fast-moving, episodic way, cutting between different times and locations. The narrative needs to be clear, but it's also important that the audience identify with Anna's psychic and emotional journey. The songs in the production, and the ticking sounds – clocks and metal striking against metal - all contribute to that journey. The music we use for the initial tango was chosen because it has a sense of size and emotionalism and fakeness that suggests Hollywood, and helps to set up the filmic quality of the piece: both the episodic structure and the film-noir atmosphere.

Voyage in the Dark in performance

Part One

Museum Piece

Darkness, within which is heard a metronomic, metallic, ticking sound. Very slowly the lights come up, gradually revealing the presence of five figures: three women, stage right, dressed in black; two men, stage left, in dark trousers and pale shirts. Slowly, rhythmically, they begin to move to and fro to the strains of a tango, their upper bodies erect, their legs making long, gliding strides. In unison their voices articulate the pulse of the tango: slow, slow, quick, quick, slow. Each figure however remains separate. Light captures individual parts of bodies: a head of glossy chestnut-coloured hair, a woman's leg extending, white and gleaming, into the playing space from the dimness at its periphery. A man and a woman begin to dance together, and are quickly divided by a second woman who enters the circle of their embrace. The remaining man and woman move towards each other and

Sphinx Theatre Company's production of *Voyage in the Dark*, 1996.
Performers: Hazel Holder (left) and Ian Kirkby. Photo: Dee Conway

are frozen in an arrested gesture of meeting. The man breaks free of their temporary suspension and, moving to stage centre, sings in a high clear voice of the dawning of love. He returns to his partner and two couples now dance, their bodies taut, elegant, needy.

The space within which they move – slowly, quickly, slowly – has a black floor and walls, and, stage right, a dull-looking mirror, behind which is imprisoned a large, dusty fan of black feathers. Across the back wall is a quite-steeply-raked walkway, suggestive of sudden entrances and surprises. The setting as a whole evokes the ambience of a museum, and, within this, the silent, stylised figures perform their strange (obsolete?) ritual. The man who sang of love moves in a circular motion around his partner. Her body is stiff: both the pivot of the man and a resriction on his free movement. He leaves her and resumes his song, which focuses now on the consequences of love – its hell that is inextricably connected to its heaven. All the dancing figures become still and join their voices to his, reinforcing the sense of ending that is integral to the process of beginning. As the song ceases everyone exits with the exception of one woman. This is Anna.

Present time, past time

Anna's first words are also the first words of Rhys's novel: 'It was as if a curtain had fallen, hiding everything I had ever known. It was almost like being born again' (Rhys 1969: 7). From the start they establish the performance's preoccupation with a dual time scheme. The curtain has fallen, the play is over, and yet Anna is 'being born', the play is begining. As Anna's speech continues, place too becomes characterised by a sense of duality. Behind the curtain, in the finished play (that will haunt the one that is now being performed), is Dominica, Anna's island home with its 'sun-heat', its characteristic scents of fruits and spices, and the sea like 'millions of spangles' (ibid.). On this side of the curtain there is cold, grey England where every street replicates every other street and the sun is a thin, fraudulent mockery of its West-Indian original. Sometimes, Anna explains, it seems to her that England is a dream and Dominica the reality, then there is a shift of perspective, a shimmer in space/time, and Dominica is the dream, England the reality. Whichever place is real, and whichever illusory, however, they remain isolated. No connection between them seems possible.

Brief comment from the future

Anna's narrative of departure/arrival is followed by a brief choric scene in which the two choral figures (two women who stand one each side of Anna) comment on the woman Anna will become: someone obliged to write to her ex-lover to ask for money for an abortion to get rid of another man's child.

Southsea

The time is October, the place the seafront at Southsea, where Anna (aged eighteen) is appearing in a show called *The Blue Waltz*. She is out walking with a fellow performer, Maudie, who is a little older than she is. Though the weather is warm for October, Anna is cold and shivery, as she always is in England. There is the sound of seagulls crying. Two men enter at the top of the walkway, pause briefly, and survey the young women. Then they saunter towards them and begin a conversation. One of the men, who has introduced himself as Mr Jones, quickly loses interest and prepares to depart. The other, Walter Jeffries, is very taken with Anna, and, prior to going off with his friend, gets her to give him her London address. The scene ends with Walter throwing wide his arms in a histrionic gesture as he assures Anna that he will look forward to their next meeting. Though he clearly means the gesture to signal the intensity of his desire to embrace that future meeting in fact it seems hollow and bombastic. Its dubious sincerity is underlined by the fact that it is held for a couple of beats, with the result that it echoes the frozen moment in the opening museum section. When Walter moves again the museum atmosphere is fully re-established. There is the sound of a slow ticking and, as the lights dim, the setting is changed by the actors who perform, at the same time, slow, dance-like movements.

Dressing room: Southsea

The place is now backstage during a performance of *The Blue Waltz*, the time soon after that of Anna's first meeting with Walter. The dressing room is indicated by three chairs, downstage, facing the audience. Seated on the chairs are Anna, Maudie and Laurie, a third member of *The Blue Waltz* cast. Anna has received a letter from Walter asking her to dine with him, and she has responded by informing him that she has a prior engagement for the day he suggests, but that she can meet him on the following Wednesday. The short scene ends with a blackout.

'Someone To Watch Over Me'

As the lights come up the actress who has played Maudie sings a brief snatch of the Gershwin song, 'Someone To Watch Over Me'. As she crosses upstage right, to exit above the glass-enclosed black fan, she passes close to Anna, who has entered in a pool of light at the top of the upstage walkway, and has stopped in an arrested position that echoes Walter's first entrance. Walter is the person who, Anna hopes, will 'watch over' her.

Sphinx Theatre Company's production of *Voyage in the Dark*, 1996. Performers: Michael Vaughan (left) and Katrina Syran. Photo: Dee Conway

London restaurant

The scene begins with Walter who is seated at a dining table, waiting. When Anna enters, he rises and helps her into a chair. As his hand touches her arm he notes the icy feel of her skin and remembers that, in Southsea, she mentioned that she was born in the West Indies. Is that why she is always so cold?

In the restaurant, secure for a while from the freezing greyness that is her perception of London, Anna describes to Walter (the desired guardian figure whom she hopes will 'watch over' her) her hot Dominican homeland. As she talks she drinks, and, the more she drinks, the faster words tumble from her mouth, conjuring up vibrant memories of the black family servants who are more real for Anna than anyone else she has known. Above all, she remembers the boatman, Black Pappy, and her special friend, Francine, whom she associates with freedom and gaiety. As she talks, however, a third figure edges her way into Anna's thoughts, someone Anna never knew but who, along with Francine, is a crucial feature of her inner landscape: an eighteen-year-old mulatto house servant called Maillotte Boyd whose name Anna once saw on an old slave-list.

When Anna comes to the end of her recital of her life in Dominica, Walter focuses on the present, questioning her about her theatre engagements and her stepmother's response to the kind of life she is leading. He has no real interest in **who** or **what** she is however. His words reveal that he views her primarily in the light of a potential sexual conquest. The lack of any genuine connection between the two of them is demonstrated when he asks her if she is, as she claims, really only eighteen and Anna's replies angrily that she can show him her birth certificate if he doesn't believe her. She has perhaps hoped, through her evocation of the black servants and friends that constitute the most real elements of her past, to open a door for him into her inner life. He, on the other hand, seeks to reassure himself of her sexual knowledgeableness, to transform eighteen from its connotations of vulnerability, and possible virginity, into a convenient fiction.

The scene ends seemingly with an impasse. Walter attempts to make love to Anna, but she angrily rejects him. Then her mood changes and she becomes sad. He is initially annoyed, then distant. Their brief embrace, with its abrupt conclusion and subsequent sense of limbo, is reminiscent of their dance movements in the opening section. A potential encounter is suspended, possibly never to be resumed. As the lights dim at the end of the scene, a clock strikes, signalling perhaps the brevity of all experience whatever its nature.

The sick room: three scenes

The setting for the three sick-room scenes – a bed – represents Anna's rented room in London. She is ill, coughing and shivering. Her landlady enters carrying a breakfast tray and an envelope which, when opened, reveals five five-pound notes and a letter from Walter telling Anna to buy herself some clothes. To the landlady the money is confirmation of her suspicion that Anna is a tart, and she tells her that she must find another room by the end of the week. When the landlady leaves the room, Anna gets out of bed, and, in her clumsy, ill-fitting petticoat, she stares at herself in the museum-like mirror, which now becomes representative of the London shop windows that simultaneously entice and reject her, beckoning her to buy, yet, at the same time, reminding her that she lacks the wherewithal to do so. With Walter's money, however, she can buy clothes, and the image of herself she will see reflected in the windows will be both desirable and desired.

The following scene is again set in Anna's room. Coughing violently, Anna is writing a letter to Walter, explaining that she is ill and asking him to come and see her. The landlady will probably not want to let him into her room, she tells him, but, if he claims to be a relative, she won't be able to prevent him from coming in. The fact that Anna is still hoping that Walter will 'watch over' her (especially now that she is ill) is emphasised by the following sequence in which Francine, the friend who watched over Anna in her Dominican homeland, makes her first entrance.

Immediately prior to this entrance, Anna recalls the heat of the Dominican sun and the light that came into her room through the slats in the jalousies. As she does so, the remembered bars of light remind her of the time when she was a child with a high fever, terrified that a cockroach in the room would fly on to her face. It is at this point that Francine enters, wearing a bright red dress – vivid and joyous like the sun – and singing softly. In a re-enactment of the past event, she kills the cockroach and then lays a wet cloth on Anna's forehead to draw the burning, painful heat out of it.

Within the London room of Anna's eighteen-year-old self, in which Francine tends the young child, Anna, a further layer of time then adheres to this interconnection of past and present, through Anna's recollection of the moment of her departure from Dominica. Again, she sees the view from the boat of the lights of the town, and feels her tears which fell, like rain, into the sea. Francine begins to exit, softly singing 'And all good times I leave behind, / Adieu, sweetheart, adieu' (ibid.: 28). Despairingly, Anna falls on her knees and clutches hold of Francine, trying to detain her. She is terrified of being left alone in the ice-world that is England. 'Being black is warm and gay, being white is cold and sad' (ibid.: 27). But Francine continues to leave. 'Adieu'; it is over. '[S]weetheart', the heart of sweetness, is no more.

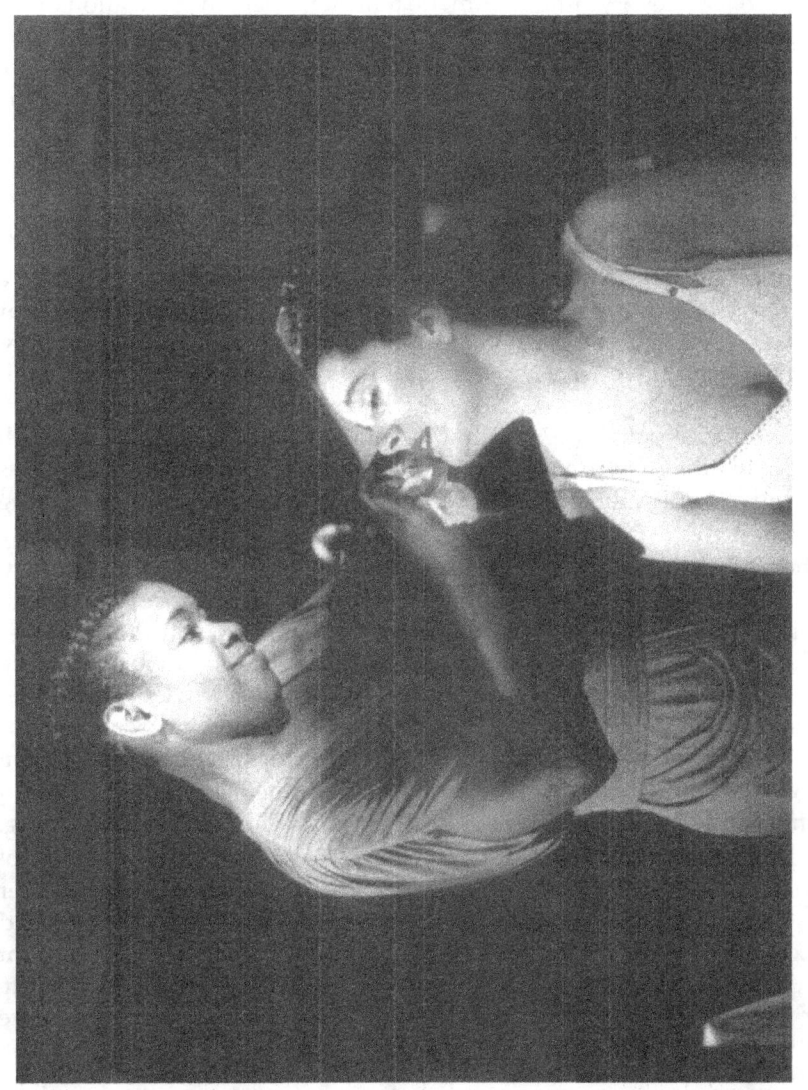

Sphinx Theatre Company's production of *Voyage in the Dark*, 1996. Performers: Hazel Holder (left) and Katrina Syran. Photo: Dee Conway

The lights dim, and, when they come up again, Anna is in bed and Walter is standing where Francine ministered to her. Speedily, he takes control, organising a warm coverlet, good food and a visit from his doctor. Anna has only to leave everything to him, he tells her. Then, in replication of his gesture at the conclusion of their initial meeting, he opens his arms wide. Rather than a lover offering reassurance, however, he looks like a clockwork toy whose body position signifies only a mechanical semblance of love, devoid of content.

Walter's house: virginity and a pink dress

In the succeeding scene, which takes place in Walter's house, Anna's assumption into a new way of life is revealed by her change of clothing, a pink dress in place of the black suit she has worn previously. Its colour provides a faint echo of the vivid red Francine wore, but, more notably, evokes English skin tones, an interpretation that is underlined by the well-cut, tailored quality of the dress which emphasises its Europeanness. Walter's understanding of Anna has developed slightly, though only with respect to **what** she is (i.e. a virgin), not to **who** she is. Their different attitudes to virginity confirm the gulf between them. To Walter it is 'the only thing that matters' (ibid. 32), a view Anna angrily rejects.

When Anna loses her virginity to Walter (loss being a crucial component of the experience), this is represented through stylised dance movement, reminiscent of the tango: Walter takes her in his arms, and then lifts her into the air while she places one leg around his body. When she is standing on the ground once again, he buries his face in her crotch while she meditates on what has just taken place between them. The act itself has been more or less what she had been led to expect by the stories she had heard from other girls, though it has been more painful than she had thought it would be. Afterwards, Walter told her not to be sad, and addressed her as darling, and it is this that stays in her mind. She longs only to remain in the state of stasis she now inhabits: past and future eradicated. When she sees Walter putting some money into her handbag she means to protest, but instead she accepts it – whatever Walter wants is what she wants too. One thought only awakens for her a sense of future time. Walter has promised to write to her the next day, and she asks him to do so soon so that she will receive the letter as early as possible.

Interim scene

Sandwiched between the first and second scenes in Walter's house is a duologue between Anna and Maudie which takes place in the new rooms

Walter has rented for Anna. In Maudie's terms Anna has done well for herself, but she needs to gain a sense of perspective on her situation – a sense in other words of the future. It's vital, Maudie comments, to remember that the relationship with Walter will come to an end, and so to be prepared to salvage what she can when the time comes. Though Anna reacts angrily to this advice the next scene, in Walter's house, shows its wisdom.

Walter's house: the 'predecessor'

Walter and Anna have recently met Walter's cousin, Vincent, and Walter asks Anna what she thought of him. Vincent can be very useful as far as her career is concerned, Walter explains, because he has contacts in the theatre world. When Anna seems unsure whether or not she wants a career, or, indeed, anything apart from being with Walter, he cheerfully tells her that she'll soon tire of him, and then goes on to talk about her 'predecessor' (ibid.: 44), placing her therefore in a long line of kept women. It is not being kept that is problematic for Anna (she wants to be in Walter's keeping), but the fact that her relationship with him is revealed as merely temporary and liable to end, as his affairs with other women have done.

The stylised lovemaking sequence of the earlier scene is repeated, but, this time, as Walter's face is again pressed to her body, Anna recalls the mulatto slave, Maillotte Boyd. Like Francine, Maillotte Boyd functions, at points in the action, as an aspect of Anna. Where Francine stands however for gaiety and warmth, Maillotte Boyd is representative of powerlessness and sexual submissiveness to a master. Anna's connection with Maillotte Boyd, and her inability to free **herself** from a slavelike mentality, is clear, when, with Walter's head against her body, she speaks Maillotte Boyd's name and then insists that the way things are the way she wants them to be. She doesn't *'want it any other way but this'* (ibid.: 48, original emphases).

Afternoon tea

From Walter's house Anna moves to afternoon tea with her stepmother, Hester, at a London hotel. In this scene, Anna outwardly rejects the black West-Indian heritage she has previously longed to claim through Francine. One of the male actors enters and reads a letter from Anna's Uncle Bo in Dominica. This leads into an angry exchange between Anna and Hester about their life in the West Indies which ends with Anna accusing Hester of implying that her 'mother was coloured' (ibid.: 56). Furiously, Anna shatters the decorum of the tearoom by screaming out her rejection of her stepmother and her values. In the future she will fend for herself. Hester need not fear that she will ask for anything from her ever again.

Savernake Forest

Having rejected the respectable white world Hester represents, however, along with the construction of her mother as 'black' – the 'warm ... gay' colour Anna supposedly admires – Anna is thrown still further on to her neediness of Walter.

Initially, this reliance does not seem to be misplaced. The tea-room sequence is followed by a scene in Savernake Forest, near a hotel where Walter and Anna plan to spend the weekend. For the first time in the play, England is portrayed as both sunny and beautiful. Warm light carpets the ground upon which Walter spreads a rug for the two of them to lie on, but the idyll is interrupted when Walter remembers that his nephew, Vincent, who is joining them for the weekend, will presumably have arrived by now. Anna will like the girl Vincent is bringing with him, Walter promises. She will find her entertaining.

The hotel

In the event, Germaine Sullivan, Vincent's 'girl', is more complex than Walter's view of her suggests. Half-French, (at least, so she claims, Walter tells Anna), Germaine speaks contemptuously of Englishmen's essential dislike of women, and their consequent inability to give them either pleasure or happiness. While Francine and Maillotte Boyd function as alter egos for Anna, respectively of her wish to partake in the gaiety and warmth she believes to characterise black people and her internalization of submissiveness towards the (white) master, Germaine represents a further aspect of Anna. Partly foreign like Anna, and, like her, from a background that others see as ambiguous, Germaine cogently articulates, and focuses, the anger that Anna could express to her stepmother only in the form of a diatribe. Anna's sense of connection with Germaine is demonstrated when she comments that she likes Germaine's views of English people. Walter, by contrast, dismisses Germaine and her criticisms, by defining her as old, despite the fact that she is the same age as Vincent.

When she is not criticising the men, however, Germaine bonds with them. She and Vincent exchange knowing glances, and laugh at Anna when she reveals the circumstances of her first meeting with Walter. Walter is irritated that Anna has allowed Vincent to pry into their affairs, but he also joins in the laughter at her expense. Angry at his mockery of her, and distressed by the unexpected information that he is going to New York the following week, taking Vincent with him, Anna stubs her cigarette out on Walter's hand. Vincent concludes the scene with the suggestion that it's time they were on their way. Whether he means that the weekend visit should be cut short, or that the relationship between Walter and Anna may be coming to an end is not clear.

Sphinx Theatre Company's production of *Voyage in the Dark*, 1996. Performers: (left to right) Ian Kirkby, Katrina Syran and Michael Vaughan. Photo: Dee Conway

'Don't forget me'

The last, brief, scene of Part One picks up on both these possibilities. The visit is curtailed and, in the closing moments of the first part, as the lights darken, Anna moves slowly towards Walter saying pleadingly, 'Don't forget me ... ever' (ibid.: 76). Her words are followed by an insistent ticking, and a low-pitched sound, muffled, distorted, premonitory. As Walter promises Anna that he will never forget her, three figures appear: one on the walkway, one by the mirror, and another stage left. Their faces are lit, their bodies in darkness. Still and silent, they transform the lovers – Anna and Walter – into museum exhibits.

Part Two

Reprise of the tango

The second half opens with a creaking reanimation of the museum creatures. The sound of a striking clock is heard as Anna walks onto the performance area from stage left. Centre stage, she pauses and looks at herself in the mirror, then exits. Tango music begins to play and, with startling abruptness, the lights come up. One after another, a man, a woman, another man, Anna, another woman enters at the top of the walkway, strikes a pose, moves swiftly on to the main playing space and begins to dance. One of the women dances between the two men, moving with both, then one, then the other. Anna dances with Walter who slides her sensuously down his body, then sends her spinning away.

A letter from Walter

Despite his promise, Walter has ended the affair, a decision he conveys via a letter written by Vincent on his behalf. The letter is spoken by Vincent to the accompaniment of elegant little dance steps. Love isn't everything, Vincent explains, especially sexual love, and the sooner that everyone, particularly girls, forget about it the better. Anna is young, and that is what really counts. Walter will of course see that she is all right for money, at least for the time being. At the conclusion of the letter, Vincent executes a neat little twirl, then adds a postscript: if Anna has kept any of Walter's letters she ought to return them.

Fragments of ghosts

Whereas for Walter and Vincent love affairs are part of the dance of life which necessitates a frequent change of partners, for Anna the end of the relationship with Walter signifies the end of life. Though she will move from man to man, her inner life is now almost entirely focused on the past,

Sphinx Theatre Company's production of *Voyage in the Dark*, 1996. Performers: (left to right) Michael Vaughan, Katrina Syran and Ian Kirkby. Photo: Dee Conway

either her West-Indian childhood and adolescence or the times she spent with Walter. Events from present time press in on her, but, though painful, they are unreal – a kind of haunting. Figures appear from the gloom, as the lights dim and then snap into brilliance. Someone places a fur coat on Anna's shoulders (a souvenir of Walter); one landlady replaces another as Anna moves from room to room; an unknown man and woman discuss Anna's situation, laughing raucously as they do so. Walter himself appears, but he seems only an effigy of Anna's ex-lover. He tells her how worried he is about her, but wants to depute the responsibility of looking after her to Vincent. As for himself, he fears that all the anxiety he is suffering will make him ill.

A letter to Walter

In Anna's London world of distorted shadows her one tangible reality becomes the letters that she attempts to write to Walter, begging for the return of his love. Page after page of paper is covered with feverish lines and squiggles, then crumpled and thrown on the floor of her latest room. A worried landlady tells her that this is no way for a young girl to live, but for Anna youth no longer has any value. She does make an effort to pull herself together. She decides that she must make a plan of some kind, and, in this way, give the insubstantial present a solid future, but, when her landlady tries to interest her in the outside world by telling her what a lovely day it is, she is assailed by memories of other lovely – now lost – days.

The landlady exits and Francine enters, herself an evocation of lovely past days, singing 'Blow rings ... Delicate rings in the air / And drift ...[oceans] away from despair' (ibid.: 90. In Rhys's novel 'oceans' is suggested as a possible solution for a missing word that Anna is unable to remember from the song.) Anna too begins to sing, her voice at first blending and harmonising with Francine's, but then, while Anna continues to sing, Francine introduces darker notes that act as a disturbing counterpoint to the melody. In a speaking, not a singing voice, she describes the Caribs, the original inhabitants of Dominica who are now exiled to one small part of the island. Then, she exits slowly, once again joining her voice in song with Anna's, and with one hand stretched back towards her, a reminder of the connection that once existed between them. Alone once more, Anna imagines herself lying motionless as 'time slide[s] past [her] like water running' (ibid.: 97). Then, mentally, she sinks down into the water, where she sees a 'face like a mask' (ibid.: 84) as she drowns.

Ethel

Anna's desperate letter writing, and her memories of Francine are followed by a sequence of scenes that chart her progress through a rackety world of massage parlours, nightclubs, and sleazy bedrooms. The scene immediately after the 'drowning' speech consists of a duologue between Anna and a masseuse called Ethel who wants Anna to join her business as a manicurist. A good-looking, young girl (youth in Ethel's view being a professional asset), Anna could charge five shillings for a manicure, as long as she is nice to the customers (who are clearly assumed to be male). Not too nice however! She should just let them talk a bit – and, if they expect more, well, that's their look-out. As she talks, Ethel is eyeing up Anna's fur coat. Eventually, she begins to touch it in order to feel its quality, and then she suggests that Anna should sell it and invest the proceeds in her business. Anna refuses, but agrees to join Ethel as a manicurist.

As the lights dim round Anna at the end of the scene, so that only she is illuminated, she thinks aloud about Ethel who has her own mechanisms of survival. Somehow, Anna too must try to survive.

Laurie

Anna's business discussion with Ethel is followed by a street encounter with Laurie (one of her fellow performers in *The Blue Waltz* at Southsea), and then by visits, in Laurie's company, to a nightclub and a hotel. Laurie has travelled to Frankfurt and Paris since Anna last saw her, sleeping with wealthy men in return for money and a good time. It's no good agonising about why Walter left her as he did, she advises Anna. It's pointless to continue to want a man who's certain to be involved in a new relationship by now. Instead, Anna should come with her to meet two Americans, Carl and Joe, who are staying at the Carlton. She still looks very young, and Carl likes young girls.

Joe

In the event it is Joe, not Carl, who sexually pursues Anna. The two Americans function as a grotesque replay of Walter and his friend, Mr Jones, whom Anna met in Southsea, the part of Joe being taken by the actor who played Walter, that of Carl by the actor who played Mr Jones. As in the Southsea encounter, the character played by this second actor leaves the company of the women prior to his friend, while, for his part, Joe becomes a distorted mask of Walter. The fact that Joe's interest in Anna will be a mocking reflection of Walter's is suggested by the words that are sung as Anna enters the nightclub: 'They're writing songs of love, but not for me', while her insubstantiality in this setting is highlighted by the fact that the dress she is wearing is Laurie's, not her own (she can no longer afford to buy clothes). It is therefore a shadow self of Anna who sits in the nightclub. The only time she speaks is in response to Carl's questioning her as to what she thinks about a woman who is looking at them disapprovingly. Anna replies that the woman is 'terrifying' (ibid. 103), causing the others to laugh at her naivety. She returns to her silent state, and the distorted nature of the scene is underscored, at its end, when a lighting change throws up a huge shadow of Joe on the mirror. His arms are extended in a way that exaggeratedly recalls Walter's two stylised open-arm gestures in Part One. He is at once absurd, theatrical and threatening.

From the nightclub the action moves to a hotel room where Anna is seen in the company of Joe and Laurie. The alcohol she has drunk serves to loosen her tongue, and she begins to quote from a poem she once found in a drawer, in one of the London rooms she has lived in, which savagely criticises the vileness of London. As she recites, she becomes increasingly sick and giddy and she has to lie down. First, however, at Laurie's insistence, she takes off her dress (so that it won't get creased), and Laurie, now reminiscent of a bawd, takes the opportunity to point out Anna's youth to Joe. Joe crosses over to the bed and takes hold of Anna's hand. Whereupon, Anna (remembering the first time Walter touched her, and his reaction to the feel of her skin, which struck him as cold and clammy) pre-empts a similar response from Joe (Walter's distorted image) by telling him that she is always cold because she comes from the West Indies. In order to try to put her in a receptive mood, Joe pretends to know the West Indies well and to have met her father. His lying mockery of her Caribbean life causes Anna once again to find her voice, and she angrily tells him to go away. In the end however Joe gets what he wants. Laurie has gone off into another room, and he begins to paw and kiss Anna. She pushes him away at first, but, eventually, as she lies inert, he falls on top of her, and lifts her skirt.

Pregnancy tango

Anna continues to see and sleep with Joe while he remains in London. Following his departure she has sex with a number of men, a development that is signalled by Joe placing a wad of notes in her cleavage, while, simultaneously, another man kisses her and a tango begins to play. Appropriately, it is while she is engaged in dancing the tango with yet another man that Anna realises she is pregnant. A sudden spasm of pain doubles her up, and temporarily deprives her of breath. When the man tries to drag her back into the dance, she bites his hand, an echo of her burning Walter's hand near the end of Part One.

The abortionist

Throughout the second part of the performance various sequences function as distorted images of events in Part One, notably through the character of Joe who grotesquely mirrors aspects of Walter. Letters too are transformed: from much-desired love-tokens into evidences of betrayal (Walter's letter

Sphinx Theatre Company's production of *Voyage in the Dark*, 1996. Performers: Anne White (left) and Michael Vaughan. Photo: Dee Conway

to Anna), or into sad and empty ghosts of what once was (Anna's fruitless attempts to write to Walter). When she realises that she is pregnant, and that she has insufficient money to pay for an abortion (despite the fact that she has now sold her fur coat), Anna begins to write to Walter once more, and this letter, with Laurie's help, is completed. Written on notepaper provided by Laurie, and in words also suggested by Laurie, Anna's final letter to Walter – a plea for the money necessary to enable her to abort another man's child – is doubly alienated from her.

As he did earlier when he broke off the affair, Walter communicates with Anna through Vincent, who now enters and agrees to fund the abortion. He insists, however, that Anna must hand back all Walter's letters in return. By the time Anna visits the abortionist, she has, therefore, been stripped of the written words of love that (however fleeting that love turned out to be) provided a degree of support in the bleak aftermath of the affair. When the abortionist begins her task, Anna's own words are erased, because they are not heard. If she is unable to stand the pain, will the woman stop, Anna asks, and, though the abortionist repeatedly cries 'yes', she does so in a shrill nightmarish tone of voice, as, like the men in Anna's life, she lifts her victim's skirt.

Carnival and a 'cold moon'

In Anna's long speech as she waits for, and then suffers, the loss of the foetus inside her, she is assailed by memories of Dominica, memories made hideous by what has happened to her in London. In place of the grinding rhythms of the tango, she hears the hot swaying pulse of a carnival procession, and, as when she was drunk in the hotel, it makes her feel sick and giddy. The grotesquely masked carnival figures remind Anna of the people she has known in England, who always seemed to be mocking her. They evoke, too, the image of the mask she saw when she imagined herself drowning, and this connection is strengthened by the smell that assails her of water and rotting leaves.

Francine enters, but, to Anna's fevered imagination, she resembles a terrifying remembered image from Dominica: a woman whose nose and mouth were eaten away by yaws. Francine's distinctive red dress translates itself in her mind into the 'red and staring' (ibid. 140) eyes of soucriants, creatures that suck one's blood, like vampires, and she imagines herself looking into a mirror and seeing soucriants' eyes staring back at her. The fearful memory of the woman with yaws dissolves, and Anna sees once again Francine, the dear companion of her childhood, but, instead of loving words, Francine mutters a curse on Anna, whom she perceives now only as white, and no longer as a friend. Exiled forever from the warmth and gaiety she associates with blackness, Anna finds herself 'alone', lost beneath a pale 'cold moon', in 'a place full of stones' (ibid.: 158). She is 'on the edge of the world' (unpublished playscript of *Voyage in the Dark*: 67), and, from there, she falls and falls.

'sweetheart adieu'

At the end of the performance a benison rests briefly on the place of stones. First, however, a doctor enters who drags Anna into an upright position on the bed and diagnoses that she will soon be 'Ready to start all over again' (Rhys.: 159). Slow, slow, quick, quick, slow: if Anna survives this time, the tango will wait to reclaim her. Walter then enters, a memory of the desire and hope that first set the tango rhythms going. He stands, motionless, some distance from Anna, lacking the power or the wish to help her. But, as Anna despairingly imagines what it would be like to begin all over again, Francine enters, in her red dress, and, standing behind Anna's bed, sings softly the words of farewell that she sang earlier in the play, 'Adieu, sweetheart, adieu'. The final mood is one of sadness and sweetness, and, to some degree, of healing as the lights fade.

Joan Wiles: the adaptor of Voyage in The Dark

I discovered Jean Rhys's work some years ago when I was given a collection of her short stories entitled Tigers are Better Looking. *I read them whilst on holiday in Nantes, where I was staying in a dirty, beautiful, old flat overlooking the square. It was an appropriate setting in which to explore the work of a writer who had spent a considerable part of her life in France. I was immediately struck by the freshness of the imagery, the musicality of the language, the startling insights, but, above all, by the intensely personal voice. Following* Tigers are Better Looking, *I went on to read the novels, and a second collection of short stories. The more I read, the more I became enchanted. I sought out any relevant material that I could lay my hands on: criticism and analysis of her work, her unfinished autobiography,* Smile, Please, *a collection of her letters, the biography by Carole Angier. I listened to radio broadcasts and amassed a collection of Jean Rhys cuttings.*

Reading her work is never a comfortable experience. The Jean Rhys woman, central to all her novels, is essentially an underdog. Down on her luck, she is exploited by, and exploits, men. She depends on the next handout, the next pretty dress, the next drink. Her world is predominantly the demi-monde of London and Paris in the twenties and thirties. There are parallels with T. S. Eliot's The Waste Land *and her characters certainly know the Prufrockian loneliness of 'restless nights in one-night cheap hotels' ('The Love Song of J. Alfred Prufrock', line 6). Victims both of time and their bodies, they drink to escape squalor, misery and despair.*

I am sometimes asked why I decided to adapt Voyage in the Dark *in preference to the other novels.* Quartet *had already been admirably adapted for the screen and produced by Merchant/Ivory. In fact, Jean Rhys herself tried to adapt* Quartet *for the stage but abandoned the attempt.* Wide Sargasso Sea *was about to receive its film première. These however were minor considerations. My ultimate choice had more to do with the nature of the novel itself. Originally called* Two Tunes *it was in fact her favourite novel. In* Voyage *we are presented with the first of her heroines. Anna Morgan, alone and vulnerable, exists in a fractured reality. The colourful warmth of her West-Indian childhood, and the cold greyness of London become dreams which she can never fit together She constantly navigates a world in which it is not just a 'difference between heat, cold; light, darkness; purple, grey. But a difference in the way I was frightened and the way I was happy' (Rhys: 7). Her passage from innocence to experience, in a society where, if you're 'afraid ... people ... see it and you're done for' (ibid.: 126), results in the spiritual desolation which haunts all her work. Consequently, Anna is not only a sympathetic character, she is also the key to a wider understanding of all Jean Rhys's work.*

Jean Rhys has always been something of an enigma in relation to other Caribbean writers. She was a white Creole, and the great-granddaughter of a slave owner, growing up as a white West Indian in a period of enormous social and political change. Her childhood in Dominica made a very significant impact on her later development as a writer. Consequently, Voyage in the Dark *has a completeness which the other novels lack. We are presented with a number of conflicts, internal and external: conflicts of the island community in terms of race, colour, sex and religion, Anna's own conflict when she arrives in London, her overwhelming sense of deracination and alienation. The other Jean Rhys women have thoughts and opinions. They ask questions about identity, illusion and reality. Anna does none of these things. Her world is a kaleidoscope of dreams and images, punctuated by people's voices, her awareness of the cold, the drabness of her surroundings, her understanding of the world and her fate, her subconsciousness. In* Good Morning Midnight *we encounter the aging Sasha Jansen, emotionally scarred and drinking herself to death. A catalogue of bitter experience has annihilated any capacity for joy. With Anna however it is her naivety, her freshness, her misguided optimism which make her story all the more poignant.*

Everything is in a constant state of flux. All connections are cut and, throughout, there is an impending sense of doom. This, together with the numerous conflicts, internal and external, had tremendous potential in terms of a theatre piece, though attempting to recreate some of the images on stage presented a challenge. I was also aware that I might not be able to do justice to what Francis Wyndham has called Jean Rhys's 'quivering immediacy'.

In Voyage *there are no logical or chronological explanations. The gaps must be filled by the reader's imagination. In order to capture the dissolution of time, which so effectively conveys the heroine's disordered experience, I used a lot of elliptical scenes, while, at the same time, trying to maintain a degree of clarity and cohesion.*

My main problem was one of structure. How could I be sufficiently selective to turn all this stream-of-consciousness material into a viable stage play? I drew up lists: of conflicts, themes, character profiles, lists of images, annotating each and every one with a page reference and cross reference. Parts of the novel proved easier to adapt than others. These I tackled first. As the scenes fell into place the structure began to evolve almost of its own volition. I had no problem envisaging Voyage theatrically, that is, I immediately found there was an interplay between my visual and auditory imagination. In other words, I could hear the dialogue and see what was happening on stage simultaneously.

Then there was the question of selection, which bits to include, which to omit. With a novel which Carole Angier describes as a masterpiece of cutting, this was no easy task. Although Voyage in the Dark charts Jean Rhys's early life in England, it wasn't in fact published until 1934, when she had achieved a degree of maturity as a writer. Consequently, her characters have a balance and objectivity which many critics believe is lacking in her earlier work. Jean Rhys's amazing ear for dialogue, combined with the perception which so accurately captures every idiosyncrasy, readily provided a cast of both colourful and complex characters. Economic constraints limited the cast to five: three female, two male. With a view to such restrictions, how many characters dare I include? Would too much doubling confuse the audience? Would they find it increasingly difficult to follow the story as Maudie lost her identity to Ethel, and Laurie became one of a succession of horrendous landladies? Just as the story has no definite chronology, the dialogue too works through a series of impressions and suggestions rather than by direct statement. As far as possible I adhered to Jean Rhys's own dialogue. On occasions however exchanges had to be fabricated to prevent scenes becoming disjointed and unintelligible. Did I have a sufficient understanding of all the characters, but above all of Anna? I placed her in imaginary settings and situations completely out of context and asked myself how she would react. When I was certain of her response I felt that I might be able to give her life on stage.

In terms of theatre, complete scenes did not present themselves obligingly on the page. Consequently, in some instances, I had to forge connections, often combining snatches of dialogue from a number of chapters, sometimes using the concluding dialogue of one scene to provide an opening for the next. In Voyage many of the scenes take place in rooms of one sort or another so the set did not pose too many problems, and images of light and darkness are so significant throughout the novel that, with Jenny Kagan's imaginative lighting techniques, the audience could immediately be transported from a seedy London bedsit to the golden warmth of a tropical island. Again, I felt the sensual quality of the writing, and the contrast, could contribute to an atmospheric piece of theatre.

Franziska Wilcken's set was inspired by Nighthawks, a painting by Edward Hopper which captures the all-pervading sense of alienation. The painting depicts *three people in a night diner. All communication is absent and, outside, the city streets are deserted. When people have left the city we are confronted with an overwhelming sense of imminent doom.*

As a stage adaptation, I felt that Voyage *had tremendous potential for exploring other art forms, particularly music and dance. Both were an integral part of Jean Rhys. Anna herself is a chorus girl when she meets Walter, and music is a fundamental part of the language of Jean Rhys. When her work is read aloud, it can have the emotional potency of a symbolist poem.*

Sue Parrish came up with the brilliant idea of introducing tango sequences. The tango is a dance which originated in the brothels of Argentina at the turn of the century as the immigrants streamed into Buenos Aires. Although they were seeking a distraction from their rootlessness and isolation, they created a music and dance that is the embodiment of pain and sorrow. The sensual nature of the choreography highlighted, and complemented, the sexual themes running throughout the play.

Voyage in the Dark *wasn't a commissioned piece. It developed first and foremost out of a passion for the writing of Jean Rhys. I sent it to the Sphinx after it had already had a four-week run at the White Bear in Kennington and was delighted when Sue Parrish said she liked it sufficiently to consider a production. Subsequently, we spent hours discussing themes, characters, Jean Rhys and the background which had contributed to so much conflict. We discussed women and self-determination in relation to class, sex, colour, religion, both in a modern and historical context. The Sphinx organised a one-day workshop, to which I was invited. Later, I was involved in casting and rehearsals involving the musician, choreographer and dialect coach. I found working with the Sphinx a very rewarding experience.*

The voice of Jean Rhys is quintessentially a feminine voice, but it also has a universality that cries out for all those who are marginalised, displaced or dispossessed. The world she depicts is in crisis. Divisions between rich and poor have given rise to an underclass and there is no safety net of social benefits. It is a world which exposes the loneliness of the human condition, where people live in fear of unemployment, homelessness, falling ill, growing old, and, as the twentieth century draws to an alarming close, is it a world so very different from our own?

Performance venues:

1996

9-27 January	Young Vic Studio	London
30 January	Gardner Arts Centre	Brighton
31 January	Lakeside Theatre	Colchester

6 February	Nuffield Studio Theatre	Lancaster
9 February	Torch Theatre	Milford Haven
14 February	Central Studio Theatre	Basingstoke
16&17 February	Playhouse Studio	Salisbury
20 February	Unity Theatre	Liverpool
24 February	QEH Theatre	Bristol
27 February	Old Town Hall	Hemel Hempstead
28 February	Arts Centre	Stamford
29 February	Millfield Theatre	Edmonton
1&2 March	Paul Robeson Theatre	Hounslow
5 March	Arena Theatre	Wolverhampton
7 March	The Gantry	Southampton
9 March	Old Town Hall	Havant

Press Quotes

'Strong and poignant production by Sphinx of Jean Rhys' 1934 novel' (Jeremy Kingston: Theatre Guide, *The Times*, 22 January 1996)

'Sue Parrish's emotionally detached and moodily film *noir*-ish production does a marvellous job at conveying the elusive themes within Rhys' haunting story of corrupted innocence.' (Roger Foss, *What's On*, 17 January 1996)

'Katrina Syran's Anna has the beauty of a Hedy Lamarr. Along with her outstanding supporting cast, she takes us into the half-world of one of the finest British writers of the century.' (Bonnie Greer, *Time Out* 17-24 January 1996)

'There is a touch of genius in which Parrish has placed the story of Anna Morgan ... in the context of the tango, that most manipulative of dances, in which the domination of the male is always challenged by the sexuality of the female'. (Peter Hepple, *The Stage*, 25 January 1996)

Sphinx Theatre Company's 1997 production of *Goliath* by Bryony Lavery, based on the book by Beatrix Campbell and directed by Annie Castledine. Designer: Kendra Ullyart. Lighting design: Jenny Kagan. Sound design: Mic Pool. Performer: Nichola McAuliffe. Photo: Simon Annand

Goliath

Credits

Performed by	Nichola McAuliffe
Directed by	Annie Castledine
Written by	Bryony Lavery
Based on the book by	Beatrix Campbell
Designed by	Kendra Ullyart
Lighting Design by	Jenny Kagan
Sound Design by	Mic Pool
Assistant Director	Bernadette Moran
Voice Coaching by	Charmian Hoare
Choreography by	Wendy Allnutt
Production Management	Alison Ritchie
Stage Manager	Jane McKeown
Deputy Stage Manager	Diane Amos
Assistant Stage Manager	Charlotte Hall
Scenery constructed by	Andy Beauchamp
Scenery painted by	Billy Jones
Exclusive tour booking management	Jan Ryan Productions
Production photography	Simon Annand
Poster/leaflet design by	Amelia Staines

'A glass conservatory, a jewel, a little piece of old England ... Now decayed and neglected...' (Kendra Ullyart, designer, from the Goliath *programme)*

Goliath in performance

Prologue

When the audience enter, the performer (Nichola McAuliffe) who will enact all the play's characters and stories is already in position, seated on a metal spiral staircase upstage centre. Dressed in black – T-shirt and combat trousers – her hair combed severely back from her face, she is very still, very focused. Around her, enclosing her and the staircase, is an old, dilapidated, but still beautiful conservatory. Faint, soft light colours the glass panes, though a number of them are broken, and all of them are dirty. Stage left, there is a long, narrrow work surface, littered with a variety of dusty objects: among them, a kettle, a crucifix, a police helmet, a milk bottle. Beneath the work surface there are boxes from which flowerpots and dead autumn leaves spill out. In the upstage left corner of the conservatory a police shield and baton are positioned. In the main area, a small step-ladder, a metal bucket and two folding chairs, one made

of wood, the other of metal and plastic, can be seen. Upstage right, is a hanging basket filled with dead-looking plants. Downstage, to the right of centre, is a metal watering can.

As the lights dim for the start of the performance, a voice is heard reciting John of Gaunt's famous speech from *Richard II*, which contains the words, 'This blessed plot, this earth, this realm, this England' (2.1.50). The woman on the stairs listens, her body intent on what she is hearing. Suddenly, the measured flow of words is splintered by sounds from a very different world. The screech of a car driven at high speed is heard, then excited Geordie voices: 'it's a red Cosworth ... / ... they're doing about 90, man ... fuck ... fuck ... Dave.../can you ... **chase** the cunts' (Lavery 1997: 2, original emphasis). Sirens wail and a police car is heard, racing after two joyriders who are in a stolen vehicle. The atmosphere is frenetic, yet oddly light-hearted. The joyriders are heading for the coast, for Whitley Bay. It's as though they are taking the police 'for a fucking day trip tonight' (ibid.), and, despite the lunatic speed, there is an almost holiday atmosphere. This is a chase, a hunt in which the quarry, along with the pursuer, willingly co-operates. Both are speed junkies, 'flying' (ibid.: 3) ever faster and faster until the speedometer moves up to a hundred and twenty-nine miles an hour. They are invincible: 'aw, man, this is the **business**' (ibid.: 2 original emphasis).

There is an appalling noise of breaking glass and metal being crumpled and torn. The joyriders have hit a lamp-post, then, as their car spins on impact, a wall. There is the sound of a huge explosion and the red glare of the burning car suffuses the upstage left area of the conservatory. Twisting herself round, so that she is looking at the audience through the metal struts of the staircase, the performer becomes Gary, one of the dead young men, and it is this character who now takes over the narrative. 'His' voice is exhilarated, adrenalin-fuelled, like those of the police we have just heard. Though the car is a mangled heap, he is still flying, streaking ahead at a hundred and twenty miles an hour. His neck breaks, his wrists and ankles come apart, his kneecaps disintegrate, but he's somewhere up above it all, floating unconcerned. The fact that he is dead is too enormous to take in.

His body corkscrews so that he is hanging by his legs. A floppy disconnected puppet without strings, he gleefully watches the scene below him. Now, someone is being pulled out of the passenger seat of the wrecked car. Momentarily, his mind focuses on who this must be, but then shies away from the realization. Nobody could pull **his** body out of the car, he boasts. He and the car are inseparably welded together. As he looks down on his body far below, he realises that the mouth is open and loud sounds are coming from it, though, at first, he can't make out the words. Then, as his consciousness re-enters the terrible mangled object in the car, a huge cry of 'Maaa ... m' (ibid.: 6) bursts from his mouth, to be echoed and re-echoed by a great roar of sound as the whole world screams for its mother.

Setting aside the character of Gary, the performer pulls herself upright and comes down the staircase as further lines from the John-of-Gaunt speech are heard.

Act One – Ely, Cardiff

The addition of a dark-coloured cardigan, and a slight hunching of the shoulders signal the performer's transformation into the first of the Ely characters, Mr Rasul. The owner of a grocery shop, who left his native Pakistan twenty-two years previously, Mr Rasul is careful, precise, filled with a strong but contained anger. Making frequent reference to a well-thumbed notebook, to ensure that he has got his facts right, he recites the catalogue of abuses that he has suffered at the hands of the locals, and which range from 'annoyance ... by youths' (ibid.: 7) to a petrol bomb that was thrown at his shop. The ostensible cause of these incidents is Mr Rasul's disagreement with the next-door newsagent, who has been selling food despite the existence of a 'restrictive covenant' (ibid.) prohibiting this. When Mr Rasul protested, the newsagent, Mr Colemmis, took his case to the Racial Equality Council – an absurd forum, Mr Rasul suggests, before which to complain about '<u>economic</u> grievances' (ibid.: 8, original emphasis). The Council's verdict has been in Mr Rasul's favour. The newsagent has been ordered to pay him three thousand pounds in compensation for the trade he has lost, and to stop selling groceries. Mr Rasul has been 'vindicated' (ibid.), though whether this will improve his position with the local community is doubtful.

At the conclusion of her speech as Mr Rasul the performer takes off her cardigan and, standing with arms akimbo, becomes Nan Colemmis, 'Nan's News'. Her ability to transform herself from one character to another is extraordinary, almost eerie. All traces of Mr Rasul seemingly disappear and she **is** the rather worn-down, initially reasonable-sounding, but increasingly aggressive Nan, wife of the newsagent. The disagreement with Mr Rasul is not racially biased, Nan confidently informs the audience. After all, her own husband's family originally came from Cyprus, so they're not likely to be racist, are they? They've just been trying to run a competitive business, and people want a choice about where they buy their bread and how much they pay for it. The verdict was unjust and there is no way they can find the money for the fine. Her husband's cousin is going around the estate, asking people to sign a petition, and her husband has put a notice in their shop window, blaming Mr Rasul for the fact that they can no longer sell food. Her voice now exultant and shrill, Nan claims that everyone sides with them, not with Mr Rasul.

Sphinx Theatre Company's 1997 production of *Goliath*. Performer: Nichola McAuliffe.
Photo: Simon Annand

A small alteration in body stance, a resumption of the cardigan, and Nan disappears and Mr Rasul is resurrected to describe the growing animosity towards himself and his family. One hot August day, he recalls, he caught a youth in the act of robbing his shop, and summoned the police by means of a switch under the counter. By the time the police arrived the youth had escaped. Then, while the police were in his shop, stones were thrown at their car and verbal abuse was hurled at Mr Rasul. The following day a hostile crowd gathered outside his shop and spat at him. The shop windows were smashed on the evening of the next day and a crowd once again gathered outside. Mr Rasul and his family had to be escorted to safety by the police.

(Mr Rasul's description of the intimidation he suffered is followed by a sequence of characters, male and female, each of whom presents the audience with a new perspective on the dangerous situation that is developing. Each one is fully inhabited by the performer for the length of time s/he holds the stage, then, through a slight adjustment in body position, and the taking off and putting on of a cardigan (which is sometimes worn around the shoulders or the waist) a new character is born.

Following Mr Rasul's 'exit', under police protection, the first character to speak is an ex-policeman, Donald Turvey. Ponderous, assured, opinionated, though at the same time very aware of the disquieting nature of the situation he is describing, he expounds the 'hardman cult' (ibid.: 12) that exists in the lower ranks of the police force. Among these men racism is endemic, and little or nothing is done by senior officers to eradicate it. As he describes this state of affairs, Donald Turvey picks up the watering can, climbs the stepladder, and waters the plants in the hanging basket. His actions evoke other retired men tending their gardens – those carefully manicured plots of green, green England – except that these plants are dead, and the water runs straight through the barren earth, denying it nurture.

Donald Turvey is followed by Sue Parry, a strung-up, hard-voiced woman who lives on the Ely estate. She is an avid supporter of 'Nan's News' and looks forward with malicious glee to the likely fate of Mr Rasul's business – 'That shop'll go up / Thass History that shop' – (ibid.), but she also provides important information about **why** the young people behave as they do. There is no other form of excitement available to them. The cinema and pool hall have closed. The youth club is hardly ever open. The estate is a desert. Though broken and desolate, it is however theirs, she claims, all they have, and **they** make the rules with regard to what goes on there, not the police or the 'Pakis' (ibid.: 14).

Ritu Barry, the next character, could hardly be more different. An Indian Brahmin, and previously an academic, she is now the local director of the Racial Equality Council. In contrast to Sue Parry, with her stabbing hand and arm movements and combative stance, Ritu is poised and elegant. Her gestures are sculptured, yet at the same time exhausted. Her explanation of her role in the unfolding events is constantly punctuated by telephone conversations as she fields requests, comments and criticisms by various Pakistani groups. Her job is to calm everyone down, to dissuade members of the Pakistani community from taking the law into their own hands. In this she is successful, but, as she ironically comments, the calm does not extend to the white community: 'We manage our angry young men./Who manages theirs?' (ibid.: 16).

The two women, Sue Parry and Ritu, are succeeded by a young man, Craig. Craig is not one of the youths who have been baiting Mr Rasul. He is likeable and uncomplicated, has been spending the day fishing, and now becomes caught up in the riot that is developing. At the moment, there is a stand-off between the youths and the police, and he finds this exciting, but in a jolly, non-aggressive way. It is a piece of entertainment, unserious and unthreatening, and it is in order to contribute to the fun that he offers his uneaten provisions from his fishing expedition around: sandwiches, crisps, chocolate biscuits. As he is unwrapping the silver foil from a biscuit, a policeman calls to him, telling him to 'put away the metal object' (ibid.: 18). He laughs. The whole thing's a gas. He hasn't got a weapon in his hand. It's just the foil from a chocolate biscuit. The police close in on him and his mood turns to one of terror. The performer uses her own hands to demonstrate Craig's head being pulled back, and fingers being pushed up his nose, as he is dragged towards the police van. With a frantic wrench of speed, Craig tears himself away from his captors and runs up the staircase, which now represents the roof of a nearby building. The sound of a police helicopter is heard, and a fierce light blinds him. At the top of his voice, he screams at his tormentors one word: 'Bastards'(ibid.: 19).

The final new character to appear in Act One is Demms Williams, the most senior police officer we have seen so far and a man well used to speaking in public. First, he carefully adjusts the creases in his trousers, then seats himself deliberately on the wooden chair, which he has placed centre stage. He is quiet, confident, fully expectant of being heard and listened to as he gives the police version of events. Only the necessary minimum of force was used, he explains, to contain the violence. The situation had escalated and it was no longer simply Mr Rasul's shop that was the target of the crowd's anger.

Demms Williams's account is followed by one more appearance by Mr Rasul. Speaking from a secret address, he narrates his and his family's terrified exit from their home, while around them people screamed abuse. Though for many years he was happy in Cardiff, he now feels it is impossible to go back there. He speculates about the way in which newspapers will present the dispute and subsequent violence, and imagines himself transformed from the butt of racist anger into 'an unreasonable trader/ [involved] in a dispute over bread'. This, he fears, is how his story will enter 'history' (ibid.: 22).

The word 'history', which brings Act One to a conclusion, reactivates the Shakespearian rhythms that were heard at the start of the performance, though this time the lines are from *Henry V* not *Richard II*. 'Now all the youth of England are on fire', a recorded voice intones, and, indeed, it seems they are, though not in defence of the realm against the French, but citizen against citizen in a chaotic and meaningless mêlée. 'For now', as Shakespeare's words appositely proclaim, 'sits Expectation in the air (Act Two Chorus, lines 1 & 8).

Act Two – Blackbird Leys, Oxford

In Act One the characters are a mixture of male and female: in Act Two they are all male. The first to appear is sixteen-year-old Andy, a minor member of a gang called the Blackbird Leys Massives. Andy wears a grey, hooded, zip-up jacket that is apparently too big for him. He is all arms and legs, and he doesn't know what to do with them. Dancing from foot to foot, his arms spreadeagled, his head bobbing like an apple on a stalk, he describes the activities of the gang: the ingenuity of the stealers of the cars, the skill and chutzpah of the drivers. **He** has performed neither of these activities. His roles are those of admirer and proselytizer. With his light, hopping movements and soft voice, which dives down on key words in his speech, he resembles a gnat, hovering in the air, buzzing, stinging.

Andy is followed, first by the Chief Constable, angry because his policing methods have been criticised, and determined to continue to take whatever measures he believes are necessary to contain the situation, and then by The Don, a driver of the stolen cars. The Don is cocksure and cool. He sports dark sunglasses and, though he is dressed in the grey jacket Andy wore, on him it fits. He pulls the hood up over a baseball cap, picks up a microphone, smiles, and launches into a rap number. This is his territory, he is the boss, The Don. What he says, goes. At the end of the song he takes a catapult from his pocket and mimes loading and firing it. Now, he is David, and the

Sphinx Theatre Company's 1997 production of *Goliath*. Performer: Nichola McAuliffe.
Photo: Simon Annand

role of Goliath is filled by the police, and by all those censorious members of the general public who try to hassle him and cramp his style.

The firing of the catapult is the incident that initiates the Blackbird Leys riot. Aimed at a police car, the missile smashes through the driver's window and out through the passenger window, grazing a police officer en route. As the constable who was in the car explains, he was lucky: he could easily have been killed. He has little sympathy for the car thieves, who have sufficient money, from somewhere, to enable them to wear designer clothes. They're not rioting because they have nothing. If his listeners have any information to offer, they should ring a special number. Slowly, he reads it out.

After the two youths and the two policemen, it is the turn of two older members of the Blackbird Leys estate to give their views. Harold is elderly and very deaf. Methodically, and with pleasurable anticipation, he lights his pipe, positions his chair upstage right, and then holds forth about the excitement of being a spectator when the joyriders start their exhibition. The lads who perform the stunts aren't dangerous in his opinion. They don't burgle houses or harm old people. What else is there for them to do? The estate was built to house car workers, but now there are no jobs. He has witnessed the police picking up a lad outside the local pub, and was disgusted by the brutal way they treated him. It was as though he was no longer in England, but, instead, in some foreign dictatorship. He also saw the catapult incident. He was out in his garden, as were his neighbours, enjoying the fun of the car display, and he saw the assailant take aim and fire. Why should this be happening now? he wonders. As when he saw the police beating the youth, the England that he thought he knew becomes displaced by an alien, bleak landscape.

Harold's view of the joyriders is contradicted by Tosh, a middle-aged man out walking his dog. As he speaks, cars are heard zooming past him constantly and he finds the noise unbearable. His nerves are like tightly-coiled wires that at any moment might unfurl. He finds it incomprehensible that parents will let their children watch the joyriders. It's not joyriding anyway in his opinion, 'it's death-riding' (ibid.: 33). His sympathies are with the police. They're doing an excellent job.

Act Two ends with a joyrider, who, with his features hidden under a balaclava, speaks as an anonymous representative of his fraternity. He picks up two large spanners and beats them loudly, first together and then on an upturned bucket, to accompany his narration of the thrill of driving stolen cars at speed. He can't make cars, as his father did, but he can drive them. His favourite model is the Maestro. It may not be 'a star', but it's his 'perfect

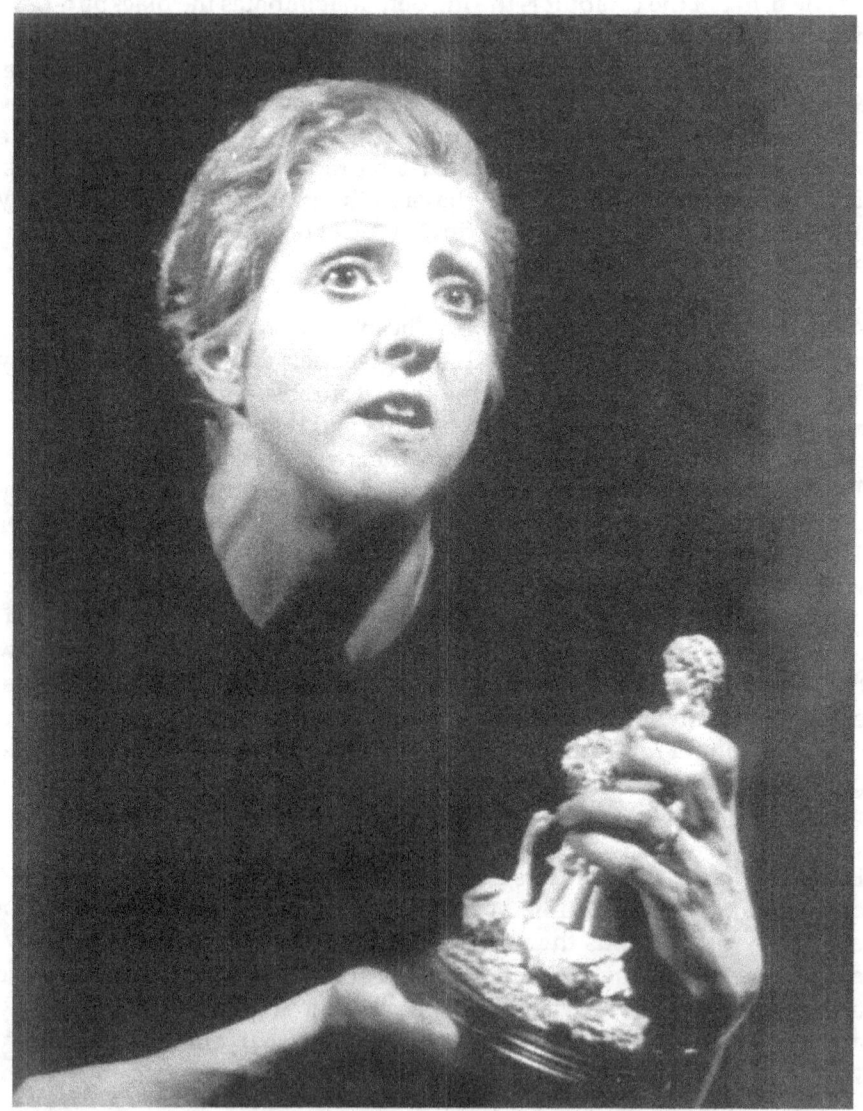

Sphinx Theatre Company's 1997 production of *Goliath*. Performer: Nichola McAuliffe.
Photo: Simon Annand

dancing partner' (ibid.: 35), and he picks up a folded chair and pirouettes with it. Then he runs up the spiral staircase, beating a loud tattoo on the metal struts as he does so. When he reaches the top, he throws his arms wide. Though his face is hidden, his body radiates the emotion which fuels his car driving: the one thing joyriding is all about – 'Joy' (ibid.: 36).

Act Three – Meadowell (Tyneside)

The patriotic strains of 'Land of Hope and Glory' are heard, at once stirring, and absurd because irrelevant. The sounds of the car chase from the beginning of the performance are replayed, ending with Gary's terrible cry for his mother, then a voice objectively relates the death of the two youths, who were so horribly mutilated in the crash that they could be identified only by their teeth. During this narration, a new character has collected a plastic binliner from the top of the stairs, and is taking out items of clothing which she throws, one at a time, down to the floor: part of a tracksuit, trainers, a football scarf. This is Gary's mother, Maureen, and she is sorting through her few remaining mementos of her son. She takes an ornament – a pottery shepherdess – from the bag and studies it closely. 'You're a lovely lass', she tells the figure, 'but you've got/"robbed" written all over you!' (ibid.: 38). Her voice is thin and weak, its tone expressive both of maternal love and hopelessness, as she remembers her birthday when Gary brought the little shepherdess home in a carrier bag. She was torn in two because, on the one hand, her son had remembered her birthday, but, on the other, his present to her was almost certainly stolen. When she pressed him about it, saying that she couldn't believe he had come by it honestly, his response was that he was 'fucking fucking off then' – and that was 'him gone' (ibid.) On the word 'gone' Maureen is overcome with grief, but she doesn't cry. Instead, she becomes very still, even more lost and defeated.

After Maureen, the next character to appear is Ruth. Capable and energetic, Ruth is a sharp-tongued woman who has no patience with the antics of the lads. Along with a number of other women, she has tried her best to do something about the miasma of hopelessness that hangs over Meadowell. In 1984 they started a Credit Union at the Advice Centre into which members put a pound a week, and could then borrow twenty percent above the amount they had saved. They've organised a Wellbeing Group, a poverty-action group and a food co-operative. For the last six years they've been going every week to the cash-and-carry, and buying basic items which they then sell to people on the estate. And, all the time they've been doing this, they've been hassled by the local lads, who've locked them into the Centre, for example, and demanded money from them with menaces.

It's only the **'lasses'** (ibid, original emphasis) who've tried to improve things. Ruth's husband just heaps abuse on her because she isn't at home looking after him and the house. He **is** at home, and could be cooking and cleaning, but he doesn't. Now a riot seems to be brewing and Ruth is frightened.

While she has been talking, Ruth has boiled a kettle and made herself a cup of tea. It is not Ruth however who drinks the tea, but a new character, Hope. Hope is an elderly black woman, and, when the audience first encounter her, she is listening to the Evening Service on the radio and singing words from 'The Song of David': the Lord is her 'shield', her 'refuge', her 'deliverer'. When she stops singing, however, she remembers the desolation outside her door and sadly concludes, 'I don't think God gets up North much' (ibid.: 42). Like Ruth, she has done her best to improve the place. She instigated a campaign to find out what the residents wanted, and, by a large majority, they voted for a play area. So that is what she and a group of other people petitioned the council for until, eventually, the necessary money was forthcoming. No money was allocated though for one essential – a 'parkie'– to keep an eye on the site. Unwilling to be beaten, the residents set up a rota and, for a year, they cleaned and protected the site themselves. Then, without prior consultation, a play worker was appointed, and the residents felt they had been disregarded. They stopped going in each week to clean the place. The play worker did his best, but he was no match for the local troublemakers, who set his hut on fire and stole from the play area, which became increasingly derelict.

Hope's words are cut short by the sounds of an explosion and glass shattering. Smoke swirls on to the stage and, in dim light, first Ruth and then Hope telephone the police and urgently describe what is going on outside: a tree being chopped down to make a barricade, a building set on fire. Interspersed with their desperate requests for help, the (offstage) voices of members of the police force who have gone into Meadowell are heard explaining that they are 'effecting a strategic withdrawal' (ibid.: 45). Also offstage, sirens scream, while, onstage, the central narrative of the riot is provided by a character who hasn't been seen before, a police officer named Rowton. A relative newcomer to the area, Rowton had been suggesting ways of defusing tension on the estate before the riot started. What was needed, he kept insisting, was a *'visible presence'* (ibid.: 46, original emphases), a few police cars driving around the estate. He was told however that, though a 'problem', Meadowell was not a 'priority', and money was available only for 'emergencies' (ibid.). This is precisely the attitude, he retorts, that creates emergencies.

Rowton's angry analysis of the police role in the build-up to the riot is followed by even more frantic telephone calls from Ruth and Hope. Ruth is watching thieves breaking into shops near her home. A petrol bomb has been thrown at a shop owned by Asians and Hope is terrified that the family may be still inside. Other telephones are heard ringing: loud, shrill, presaging disaster. In furious despair, Rowton asks how he will be able to tell the police under his command to 'be caring ... after this' (ibid.: 47). How, too, will the people on the estate ever see beyond the uniforms, and realise that the police are similar to themselves? The situation seems hopeless.

(Rowton will appear again at the end of the performance but first, in turn, Ruth, Maureen and Hope speak. As each of them does so, she holds an object which is part of the story she narrates. Ruth has a bottle of milk that she had just been out to buy when she first became worried about the number of lads thronging the streets. Maureen has an 'eternal-bow' teapot, given to her by her son on her wedding anniversary, and Hope has her Bible.)

Ruth is illuminated by a 'tiny light in surrounding darkness' (ibid.: 48). It was the pensioners' Bingo Night, she explains, when she went to buy the milk and noticed the gang of lads. Near the shops she saw elderly men weeping out of fear and bewilderment, and everyone was asking where the police were. Then, they saw a helicopter observing them from high above, and, a bit later, policemen appeared on the estate. They were dressed in riot gear and carrying truncheons, and they jumped out of their vans and began beating two lads who had played no part in the riot. The women tried to intervene, but the police called them 'Sluts' and told them, in a foul-mouthed way, to get inside their houses. The aggression was totally unnecessary, Ruth tells the audience. Nobody was being cheeky, or panicking. They were too frightened. They just did as they were told.

Maureen's story is about the incident that first made her realise the pull that the life of the streets was exerting on her son, Gary. One night, when he was ten, Gary took some money from her purse and said he wanted to go for fish and chips. At first she told him that it was too late, but, then, when he kept on asking, she gave in, saying that he must be back by ten. At this point in the story she smiles fondly, remembering that, to her amazement, he actually was home by that time, but then her expression changes as she remembers what happened next. She was sitting in a chair, with Gary standing behind her, and she asked her husband what he was doing. Her husband laughed. Gary was holding an imaginary knife and using it to stab his mother's neck.

After this he became genuinely violent towards her. He also began to play truant from school. So she took him along to see the headmaster, but all the headmaster did, when Gary said he wasn't staying, was to point him to the door.

Maureen has placed the metal bucket centre stage. Now she begins to tear up Gary's school exercise books and, as she puts the pieces in the bucket, she recalls her own attempts to educate her son. She taught him all that she knew: reading, writing, telling the time. She did her best. 'Bloody school didn't' (ibid.: 51), she adds bitterly, at the same time setting fire to the torn paper in the bucket.

Last year she saw Gary breaking into their own local newsagent's and she 'phoned the police. She grassed her own son, because she knew no other way of getting help for him, but it didn't work. He was constantly in and out of prison.

Hope's story is from the Bible. By what faint light remains, she reads aloud the exploits of David and Goliath, then ponders their meaning for her. The figure of Goliath she recognises – his activities are evident all around her – but what about David? Is there any hope that he will come and rescue them? She weighs the two names against each other, and decides that there is no difference between them. David, Goliath: they're both 'the same./ Lads with bricks' (ibid.: 53). All her life she has trusted in God, but now she knows that God is like everyone else. He cares nothing for women, or for the poor. As she fearfully contemplates her loss of faith, there is a huge explosion. Meadowell ignites. The whole world it seems is ending.

Aftermath

As light returns, Rowton is standing centre stage and it is this character who provides the final narrative of the Meadowell riot. Once things had calmed down, he expains, he despatched women officers into Meadowell, whose role was to pick up what pieces remained in the aftermath of the violence. The place resembled a war zone. He accompanied a group of women officers to the Community Rights Centre, and, to their amazement, they found that the electricity was still working. So the women made tea, and people began dropping in. They were shocked and frightened, but at least there was someone to talk to about it.

For the next two weeks, the police interviewed residents on the estate, but they got little for their pains. People blamed the police as much as they blamed the lads. The problem was compounded by the fact that an evidence-gathering device that should have been put aboard the helicopter on the night of the riot had somehow been forgotten about, and so there was 'no independent police corroboration' (ibid.: 56). Rowton's glad that he will be retiring soon. His son has opted against a police career and Rowton thinks this is for the best. He'd like to see the young man somewhere 'where he can be ... '. He searches for the apposite word, and eventually locates it: 'effective' (ibid.). He thinks again of the devastation in Meadowell, and finds himself remembering the words of Marriott Edgar's poem 'The Lion and Albert', in which, after Albert is eaten by the lion, the Magistrate gives his 'opinion', which is 'That no one [is] ... really to blame', and he hopes that Albert's parents will have 'further sons to their name'. Albert's mother's furious words are also the final ones of the play:

"And thank you, sir, kindly" said she,
"What, waste all our lives raising children
"To feed ruddy Lions? Not me"!!! (quoted in Lavery: 57)

It is almost, though perhaps not quite, an impasse. Miraculously, the electricity still works. The women are offering tea and sympathy (as always), and Rowton is doing his best, but the Goliath of lack of opportunity and hopelessness seems as great as ever.

(This description of the play in performance relates to the text as it was played at the Bush Theatre in London. Prior to this, the order of speeches in Act Three was slightly different. In place of Rowton there was a woman police officer, and it was this character who ended the piece by reading William Cowper's lines beginning, 'England, with all thy faults, I love thee still' She then stood for a few moments, 'thinking, uncertain [before she left] the riot-torn area' (*Goliath*, unpublished script.: 58). The substitution of Rowton and the use of the Marriott Edgar quotation are discussed by Bryony Lavery in the following section.)

Bryony Lavery

The following comments by Bryony Lavery were taken from four separate interviews, (four stages in the *Goliath* project), the first early in the work process, the second shortly after a two-week workshop in the course of which the basic structure of *Goliath* was established, the third after the show began to tour, and the final one while it was playing at the Bush Theatre.

Stage One: Beginnings

Starting point. *The initial idea came, I think, from Annie Castledine who had been inflamed by a passion for the work of Anna Deavere Smith after seeing her one-woman show,* Fires in the Mirror, *at the Royal Court. Annie wanted to create a piece in a similar frame, based on Beatrix Campbell's* Goliath. *She asked me if I* was interested in writing it, and it seemed such an impossible idea that I wanted to do it in order to find out how to do it. I was less certain about Anna Deavere Smith's working method of compiling a large number of interviews and then shaping this material to create a show, because doing interviews isn't really my style. I'm a fiction writer. It soon became clear though that everyone involved in the project was too fiction-imbued to follow the Anna-Deavere-Smith method closely and we decided instead to create a fictional piece that would reflect the experiences recounted in Goliath. The characters would be based on Bea's book, but would be created by Annie, and the performer, and myself in response to a story.

Present stage of the project: In my first draft I've adopted what is for me a relatively new work method, which is – where there are bits I can't quite work out – to just to put them down anyway (for the time being). The first draft includes attempts at things. I've got five choruses, like in Henry V, because it seemed to me that the subject matter is a war, and Bea is talking about the unheralded and unsung achievements of women. So that's what I've started with.

At the moment I'm working on the second draft, and what we think is going to happen is that it will start with a terrific car chase. The audience will hear the car chase and will know that two youths in the car have possibly been killed. My idea is that somehow we're going to create a smashed car on stage, and that this car is going to reconstitute itself as armour covering one of the dead youths, who will then allow all the voices of the women to speak.

Davids, Davidas, and Goliaths: There are really two teams of Davids, the lads on the estates and the police lads, who, as Bea says, are not a lot different in type and kind from the ones chucking the stones. There are also a number of Davidas: the book is about any number of heroic women. In the Bible the account is all about the men's struggle – as it is in Henry V. The women in Goliath have no weapons, apart from little stories of persistence and good will, and they're defeated over and over again by the Goliaths of everything else, but they're heroic nevertheless. There are so few theatrical representations of grand courage by women – Mother Courage is a sort of back-door entry into the idea, in that it's about war, but her courage is of a different order – and I think that it follows from this that the production values should be very high. The subject should be treated with glory, to make the point that the women's struggles in these areas are as great and worthy of grandeur as Henry V's fight. In Bea's book the women's words and actions, and Bea's account of these actions, show how heroic their response is to a huge Goliath of circumstances and problems. She understands the heroism, and I'm trying to find the stage picture to represent that.

Stage Two: Reflections on the two-week workshop (by this stage the performer, Nichola McAuliffe, was involved, along with Bryony Lavery, Annie Castledine, the director, and the designer, Kendra Ullyart)

Developments to the script: *It still begins with the police giving chase to a stolen car and then the car exploding. The next thing is a monologue from the dead boy. We've given up the idea of the smashed car reconstituting itself into armour. It would take up too much of the budget, and, anyway, it isn't necessary. One person is performing all the characters and she's a woman. She carries all the voices – they drop into her – so we don't have to obviously make the connections that we would have to if there were several performers.*

The various characters' voices establish their stories, and that's what the book, Goliath, *is all about – the abandonment of the estates and their residents by government, and also the disenfranchisement of youths with no jobs, which, spookily enough, is taken more seriously than the disenfranchisement of women with no jobs.*

*The order of the piece now is the Prologue, in which the dead youth speaks, and that's sheer flying testosterone – the joy of "Wow! I hit something at a hundred and twenty-three miles an hour and I've come apart. Isn't it amazing!" The Prologue is all male voices, then the three acts focus on each of the three estates. Ely is a mixture of men's and women's voices, Blackbird Leys is all men and Meadowell is all women. Finally, we return to hearing the police give chase and, by then, it will be clear what's happened and **why** these things happen.*

Reactions to the performer: *Nichola is so talented that I feel that there's nothing she can't try. Her skill with accents is extraordinary: she can do three or four different shadings of a basic accent. In the workshop she did, for example, a Pakistani/ Welsh shopkeeper, a black Meadowell woman with a Geordie accent, and two or three other different Geordies. In earlier drafts of the script I moved between the three locations (rather than keeping them separate), because it never occurred to me that Nichola would be able to differentiate so clearly between characters, but I'd catered for something I didn't need to cater for. I don't have to worry about creating a structure where characters from the same region speak one after the other.*

Production values/the set: *Over the two weeks of the workshop it's become clear that everyone has high production values. One day we had what was called a design day. Kendra talked about how she started working on a design – the kind of structures and feelings from which she began. Annie had an image of a kind of conservatory and I had in my mind the phrase 'where urban meets rural', because most of the places that are talked about in the play are on the edge of the country. This fact amazed me when I first discovered it. I visited Meadowell, and it was bleak, bleak, bleak – urban waste and very sparse grass – but it was surrounded by Northumberland, and County Durham was quite near. Blackbird Leys is in lush Middle England. I haven't been to Cardiff recently, but there's a similar pattern there.*

Stage Three: Goliath in performance

The set: *When the set came it was both beautiful and a realization of what we'd discussed in the workshop. It was absolutely right – a divine leap to an appropriate metaphor. Its fragility, and the broken glass in some of the panes, suggested the fragility of society, and the iron and wood of which it was made evoked years and years of British industry. From an acting point of view it's ideal, firstly for props, because you can bung any old thing in a greenhouse, and, secondly, because it has a variety of different playing spaces. There's the place where Nichola makes tea, for example, and the staircase. I think the set is a triumph.*

Police response to the production: *Nichola has a lot of connections and friends within the police force, and she's been responsible for a good number of police seeing the show. Some of them came over from Chapeltown (in Leeds) to Liverpool, for example, with a number of kids. She got a letter from the police afterwards saying that, at first, they'd been against it, and felt that the police were shown as stupid, but then they thought about it further and realised that it wasn't so. One high-ranking police officer, who came to see it on the first night, was chiefly struck by the fact that, as he said, "Nobody talked to each other". Of course, because there's only one person on stage the characters can't talk to each other, but the whole thing is about lack of communication, and the fact that there's only one person reinforces that.*

The show has had a big effect on the police who've seen it.

Stage Four: Retrospective, new developments, comparisons with More Light

Retrospective on the work process: *Looking back, the work process started off quite feisty and tricky, but I think this was because we were finding, and understanding, one another's language. We've developed a very comfortable and confident exchange of knowing who's doing what role. There's an understanding that somebody's doing the main body of writing and this can then be added to and improved. Nichola, for example, has done some wonderful rejigging of speeches. I've sometimes seen writers (especially young writers) getting really blind in their heads when actors chipped in with suggestions because there were too many people involved, or the writer wasn't ready to cope with this input. But I've found it very helpful on* Goliath.

Annie (Castledine) has steered the structure and the style hugely, and Goliath *has finally become a prime example of a very good director working on a new piece of work in an appropriate manner. She's inexorable about getting the right shape – and* Goliath *is her shape in a way.*

It's such a meshed piece now, so organic, that, when somebody compliments me on the writing, I feel that we should be complimented as a group.

Changes to the final section: (a) a new police officer – *The woman officer, Joan, who used to end the piece was a weak link. We'd decided that Act Three should be all women's voices, and this was an honourable decision, but in the end we needed someone with more authority as the final voice. Rowton, the new character, is interesting because he really grasps the situation. The other police characters are largely involved in damage limitation, whereas Rowton provides a more complex perspective. He understands the police situation and its heartbreak. He takes over Joan's role of describing the women police officers going into Meadowell, in the aftermath of the riot, to try to offer assistance, but, in contrast to Joan, he is able simultaneously to present this action from three reference points. There is the viewpoint of the women themselves, then that of the force, who perceive women as naturally suited to this type of role, and, finally, there is Rowton's own realization of the irony of that perception – the fact that it keeps everything in its place, as it has always been, because it doesn't give women credence for anything else.*

(b) 'The Lion and Albert': *Annie and I were going through possible rewrites for the Bush and suddenly I knew that it would be a good idea to use the end of 'The Lion and Albert' to conclude the show. It was purely instinctive, but, of course, instinct is based on very solid things. I think it makes absolute sense because it's working class. It's very good working-class poetry.*

Goliath in the changed political climate (*following the Labour victory in the 1997 General Election*): *I had quite an anxiety that the change of government would make the show feel old-fashioned, but it doesn't at all. If anything, it seems to have had a greater effect. Tom Clarke was in the audience last night, and it's the first time that a member of the government has come to see a show of mine. I think the fact that he was there is important. The show exists as a benchmark to what must be improved and taken on, and, I think, as a piece of theatre, it works better because there's a possible answer to the despair.*

Comparisons between Goliath and Bryony Lavery's play More Light (More Light *was one of the twelve plays commissioned by the Royal National Theatre for the BT National Connections scheme for young people in 1997. These plays received a number of productions throughout Britain. Twelve of the most interesting productions were then performed on the Olivier and Cottesloe stages at the National Theatre in July 1997.*): *It's been very interesting working on* Goliath *and then watching a production of* More Light*, which was written for nineteen women, and, in the production at the Olivier, was played entirely by boys.* Goliath *has a cast of nineteen characters, all played by one performer, and both productions have rocked my notion of who should play what on stage. I used to be furious about men taking women's parts, because there aren't many parts for women, but, if people were cast according to ability rather than gender, the work would be so interesting. I have two examples of work which I know are fascinating. The entire Olivier* *audience watched the boys in* More Light, *who were aged from about thirteen to eighteen, watched with very specific attention, and, in* Goliath, *Nichola plays all genders and colours. We rarely challenge the naturalistic assumption that women should be played by women, and men by men, and it's so dull.*

I also learned from the production of More Light *that you can put anything into a theatre piece regardless of who's going to perform it. I didn't write* More Light *for children. It's a heavy piece, with sex and cannibalism and castration in it. The director of the (boys school') production that was chosen for performance at the National was worried initially about whether he'd get the play past the staff at the school, and yet it was selected for a showcase at the National. I went to see it and it was extraordinary. It got a standing ovation, and it deserved it. And then I got a standing ovation, and I deserved it. The boys played women, and men – and it doesn't matter, unless it's unfair.*

I don't quite know what to do with this knowledge, but I do want to use it in some way. I've always found fourth-wall acting peculiar and I've suddenly realised that I find people playing their own genders as peculiar, and stuck, and dull, and limiting.

The writer's role: *I think I'm writing very well at the moment. It's as if the hard work is paying off. Sometimes your work is vulnerable, and sometimes it's strong, and there isn't a particular reason why this should be so, apart from public opinion. It's nice to be in a confident position, but strange because it's one's job to be on the fringes of society, pointing out its flaws. To find oneself being agreed with is a little disconcerting. I don't want to be part of the Establishment.*

Performance Venues:

1997

13-22 February	Gulbenkian Studio Newcastle Playhouse	Newcastle
25 February-1 March	West Yorkshire Playhouse	Leeds
3&4 March	Emlyn Williams Studio Theatr Clwyd	Mold, Clwyd
5-8 March	Sherman Theatre	Cardiff
10-15 March	Ustinov Studio Theatre Royal	Bath
18-22 March	Leicester Haymarket Studio	Leicester
26&27 March	The Theatre	Chipping Norton
4&5 April	Hull Truck Theatre	Hull
9-12 April	Traverse Theatre	Edinburgh
15-19 April	Everyman	Liverpool
22 April	New Theatre Royal	Portsmouth
24-26 April	Warwick Arts Centre	University of Warwick
23 July-16 August	Bush Theatre	London

Press Quotes

'For sheer hit-you-between-the-eyes impact you would have to go a long way to find better than this production.' (Quentin Clark, *The Stage*, 3 April 1997)

'McAuliffe is a one-woman acting masterclass ... A Goliath of a play indeed, and a truly magnificent performance.' (Lizz Brain, *Leicester Mercury*, 20 March 1997)

'Directed brilliantly by ... Annie Castledine, Ms McAuliffe is breathtaking ... It's the performance of the year so far.'(Bill Hagerty, *News of the World*, 3 August 1997)

'a striking and serious work which shows off an actress at the height of her powers' (Nick Curtis, *Evening Standard*, 4 August 1997)

AFTERWORD

The six productions documented in this book were randomly chosen inasmuch as they were the theatre pieces the companies were working on during the period of my research. In the process of working on the book, however, it became increasingly clear to me that, despite their apparent differences, the pieces exhibited a number of similarities both structurally and thematically. In particular, I was intrigued by a frequent focus on characters who inhabit limbo worlds (ways of being, and sets of perceptions that inhibit forward movement), and, additionally, by a preoccupation with what I will call the concept of 'the two' (two worlds, two linked characters).

The structural and thematic importance of 'the two' is most obviously evident in *Boadicea* where the two worlds, the two sisters, and the two names (Boadicea/Boudicca) are integral to interlinked ideas the piece explores: 'voice' and silence, and possible reactions by women to male violence. The two sisters, Voddiccia and Voada, embody opposed ways of responding to rape, Voddiccia enacting a desperate and ghastly form of vengeance, while Voada elects to become silent. The fact that this silence is self-chosen is important. Unlike her literary forebears, Philomela in Ovid's *Metamorphoses* and Lavinia in *Titus Andronicus*, Voada's tongue is not cut out by her attacker, and she does not therefore suffer what Elissa Marder in 'Disarticulated Voices: Feminism and Philomela' (*Hypatia* 7, 2: 148-66) defines as a second and 'symbolic' rape which deprives the victim of a language through which to express her violation. Philomela and Lavinia are forcibly silenced, but Voada's dumbness results from her witnessing of her mother and sister in the act of cutting off the breasts of the Roman mothers and sewing them to their lips. Herself pregnant, she identifies with the mutilated women. Their sealed and bloody mouths stitch up her lips too.

Though only a child herself, Voada chooses to accept her given role of nurturing mother. Through this decision she becomes part of another 'two', this time with her mother, Boudicca, as the opposed element. After the rape of her two daughters, Boudicca prays to the goddess, Andarte, for aid in the revenge she plans on the Romans, beseeching the goddess to 'Destroy [her] mother heart, so that [she] can avenge [her] children' (B.:12). To claim her right to a mother's vengeance Boudicca must refuse the role of compassionate mother. Motherhood is therefore revealed as double, consisting, as it does, both of the nurturance with which Voada allies herself and the destructive capability, embodied in Andarte, that Boudicca emulates.

By means of her invocation of Andarte, Boudicca transforms herself into a pitiless war machine, while the tender aspects of her maternity become infused into the magic life-stone. Voddiccia describes this stone as being 'full of weak things', but, to Voada, 'It's full of love' (ibid.). Later, in the Netherworld, Voada briefly reclaims her voice in order to tell the story of 'Big Stone and Little Stone', which casts Big Stone (Boudicca) as a monstrous mother. As she tells the story, Voada holds in her hand the life-stone which represents the view of motherhood to which **she** is committed.

Voada also functions as an opposite of her mother through her elected dumbness. As Celtic culture was non-literate, the events of Boudicca's life, and the details of the final battle have come down to us through the words of the victors. The Iceni, of whom Boudicca was the leader, were silenced, both through their military defeat and through their inability to write their own version of events. In the Netherworld of *Boadicea* the eponymous protagonist decides to redress this imbalance. While Voada, who **can** speak, chooses not to, Boadicea, who is unable to speak on paper, finds someone to do this for her. Marius has learned how to write during his time with the Romans, and he notes down the story Boadicea concocts – 'concocts' being the operative word, for the version of her past the Red-Bellied Queen articulates is hollow and bombastic – in Voada's words, 'lies, omissions and fantasy' (*B*.: 15). The immediacy of the horror of the rape, and the terrible vengeance Boudicca and Voddiccia have exacted, become not only simplified but also traduced. Above all, the counterpoint of Voada's resistance to the atrocities committed by her mother and sister is lost. Self-silenced in the Pastworld, Voada is ignored in the Netherworld.

Both Past and Nether worlds move finally to the ultimate battle, the battle that for a long time in the Netherworld Boadicea believes that she won. The piece ends in the Netherworld where Boadicea finally remembers correctly what happened: eighty thousand Celts were massacred. Her last words, 'Falling, falling, falling. Over and over' (*B*.: 21), locate Boadicea/ Boudicca and her daughters within the final, and defining, moments of their lives. Eternally, Boadicea/Boudicca falls, gets up, falls, gets up. Voddiccia kills her mother – she 'had to do it' (ibid.) – then sits bereft and alone, without a role to play once that of avenger has gone. Still vocally silent, Voada finds a voice through her music, her violin crying out its threnody of loss.

In the Netherworld scenes of *Boadicea* the characters seek a perspective from which to view their past. What they achieve is a reactivation of the culminating point of that past, plus, in the case of two of the characters, a simultaneous commentary on it. Boudicca/Boadicea is both defeated and resists defeat. Through her music, Voada mourns not only the massacre of her people, but, in addition, the extinguishing of her unborn – half-Roman – child. The end of the piece, like its defining structures, is therefore double;

the characters both gain a degree of distance from events and remain stuck within them.

Different as is its subject matter from that of *Boadicea*, *Voyage in the Dark* is likewise concerned with images from a past world. Additionally, it too has its nether world, for the twentieth-century London Anna inhabits has the submerged quality of a shadowy underground cavern. Within her netherspace Anna is visually aware of her vibrant light-filled Dominican past world, and is haunted by a variety of potential doubles of self: warm, lifeenhancing Francine (the person she longs to be), the slave girl, Maillotte Boyd whom she resembles in her sexual submissiveness to Walter, and the woman with yaws whose eaten-away face and red, staring eyes Anna is terrified will stare back at her from the mirror. Wherever Annna turns she catches glimpses of her Dominican life, and, in the second half of the play, also of her later life with Walter, but the present is a landscape she rarely fully enters. In *Voyage in the Dark* past and nether worlds exist simultaneously yet apart.

In addition to the two co-existing worlds and the importance of doubleness in the play, *Voyage in the Dark* resembles *Boadicea* in that, at the end, Anna, like Boadicea, falls and falls, in her case into a wilderness of desolation. Though the play ends with Francine's valediction, which is also a song of love, the image of the lost and falling Anna complicates this tenderness. Unlike Boadicea, Anna does not get to her feet after she falls. In Jean Rhys's original version of the novel Anna died. In the published text, which the Sphinx production followed, she survives – in a sense. In the words of the doctor who attends her after the botched abortion, she will soon be 'Ready to start all over again' (Rhys 1969: 159), but, as it is presumed that this restarting will simply lead Anna back to the place where she is now, death is only temporarily held at bay. While Boadicea's 'falling falling. Over and over' is to some degree counterbalanced by her repeated struggle back to her feet, Anna's starting 'all over again' will be dictated by the tango rhythms of desire over which she has no control.

Like *Boadicea* and *Voyage in the Dark*, *The Sisters* is constructed around two worlds, in this case a past the sisters inhabit in memory and a present that is the theatrical 'now' of performance time. The sisters themselves experience the present very much as does Anna in *Voyage*, as a shadowy presence on the edge of consciousness, but, in *The Sisters*, the constant presence of the nurse-cum-presenter figure, Anfisa, invites the audience to look objectively at the sisters as well as to sympathise with them. In contrast to *Voyage*, which begins, as it essentially continues, with the voice, and from the perspective of Anna, *The Sisters* opens with Anfisa announcing the start of the performance and tracing out on the playing area the spatial patterns that will distinguish it. *Voyage* too has its ongoing choreography, but this is dictated by the rhythms of the tango which seduce the audience along with Anna. In *The Sisters* the rigid parallel and diagonal lines of the characters' movements create a physical grid that acts as a reminder for the audience of the ritual in which the sisters are engaged. The audience are invited both to enter into the world of memory and to bear in mind the fact that they are watching a performance.

The doubleness of response *The Sisters* encourages is closely related to its central concern, which is a ritualised replaying of the past in an attempt to escape from that past. While Anna longs to be at one with the past, and Boadicea and her daughters desire both to reclaim the past and to find a perspective which will give them a handle on it, the sisters want to want to escape from desires that hold them in thrall. (This double use of 'want to' highlights the near impossibility of their quest because what they desire is the desire to forget desire. 'Moscow' can only be reimagined if the past becomes truly past.) It is in order to try to find a point of departure from the past world that Anfisa has conjured up the theatrical 'now' that the sisters perceive as a limbo-space, neither fully past nor fully present (a kind of netherworld), even while they partly realise that they need to enter its immediacy. The physical entities with which they engage there, notably the window, are for them almost exclusively signifiers of past events, though the audience's attention is also drawn to their role as stage objects. In a similar way, the audience perceive the characters' patterned movements and gestures as simultaneously remembrances of things past and actions within present space and time.

This focus on the given circumstances of performance, along with those of Chekhov's play world, gives rise to speculation as to the place in which the sisters would find themselves if the ritual succeeded and they escaped from their unrealistic dreams. Would they rewrite the ending of *Three Sisters*, or would they find themselves on a stage confronting an audience, and, if so, what would the nature of that encounter be: character to audience, actor to audience? These questions are unanswerable. The point of *The Sisters* **is** the ritual, the quest for escape. Once that were achieved, the piece would be over. Given the importance of ideas of victimization and loss in *Boadicea* and *Voyage*, however, it is noteworthy that a direct engagement with these ideas by the sisters would end the performance. In *Voyage*, by contrast, Anna's sense of victimization and loss is not subjected to criticism. In the final moments of *Boadicea*, Voada highlights the importance of **remembering** loss, while, through her elected dumbness and acquiescence in her given maternal role, she, to some degree at least, reimagines and reclaims victimhood.

While the sisters by and large remain imprisoned within memory despite Anfisa's efforts to free them, the characters in Scarlet Theatre's *Paper Walls* succeed in escaping from the external violence that has been the defining factor of their lives to date. In the first half of the piece this violence is presented through fragmentary signs the audience has to try to interpret: a finger writing on the smeared glass of the window, for example. A message, yes, but is it meant to be taken seriously, or is it a joke? In the second half the past is replayed but now the shed (house) has been opened up, the past effectively turned inside out.

These two versions of the past, the outer and the inner, are bridged by the first appearance of the dolls, the miniature replicas of the characters. Before the doubling back on the past is enacted, therefore, doubles of the women appear in order to prepare for this possibility. Beautiful, but weirdly ghostlike figures, the dolls embody a disturbing otherness that has similarities to the remnants of her Dominican past that haunt Anna in *Voyage*. Whereas Maillotte Boyd, the woman with yaws, and even Francine, link Anna to the ancestors who took violent possession of the island and its people, however, the dolls are the means by which the women free themselves from a violence of which they have been victims. The doll-women enable the actual women to transform the doll's house that has served as their gaol. The tools with which they have been forced to maintain their prison become their means of escape, the giant saw (its size mocking the puniness of their unseen gaoler) ripping the walls apart as though they were literally made of paper.

In Foursight Theatre's *Slap* the imprisoning forces from the past are institutional and ideological and the new relationship that is forged with the past is achieved gradually, in contrast to the violent severance that takes place in *Paper Walls*. As in *Boadicea*, there is a strong focus on mother/daughter interaction, used here to create the links between past and present. Though Shauna and Theresa both reject aspects of their pasts (Shauna her Catholicism and Theresa domicile in Northern Ireland), *Slap* depicts both a progression and a reclaiming. Theresa affirms many of the values her grandmother lived by, while rejecting the authoritarianism that underlay them.

Given its focus on three generations of women, doubleness is less obvious in *Slap* than it is in the other pieces. However the fact that all three characters are played by the same person creates a sense of replication, which is reinforced by the sequences in which the daughter retells a story earlier narrated by her mother, her bodily position at times echoing that of the older woman. The moments when, first Shauna, and later Theresa, adopt physical attitudes reminiscent of Gracie's when she has her vision of the Virgin Mary act as further links between the women (each of whom is an actual or expectant mother as well as a daughter), and, additionally, underline their various responses to the Catholic Church's ideal of the perfect mother. Gracie prays to the non-sexualised Mary for help in surviving the effects of undesired sexual encounters. Shauna and Theresa both reinvent the image of the Virgin Mother, Shauna through her embodiment of a sexualised maternity in relation to the soldier, and Theresa through her alternative interpretation of virginity.

In *Goliath* the idea of the two is continued through the related images of David and Goliath, and also through the fact that both the lads from the estates and the police 'lads' can be characterised as Davids. The existence of the Davidas provides a further elaboration of this concept. Like *Slap*, *Goliath* consists basically of three sections, each one based, in this case, in a different location rather than a different time. In contrast to *Slap*, and also to *Paper Walls* and *Boadicea: The Red-Bellied Queen*, in *Goliath* there is a focus on the mother/son, rather than the mother/daughter relationship.

The imprisoning forces in *Goliath* – the Goliath itself, in fact – are poverty, unemployment, lack of opportunity, the denial of the right to be listened to. The limbo-lands inhabited by the Chekhovian sisters, by Anna in *Voyage in the Dark*, and by the characters in *Boadicea* have spread in *Goliath*, so that they now embrace whole communities. Despite *Goliath*'s biblical title, however, these nether worlds do not have their origins in fictional or legendary narratives (as was the case with the three above-mentioned productions), but in a documentation of actual recent events. At the end of *Goliath*, the senior police officer (Rowton) cogently articulates the problems that led to the riots. No way forward can, however, be demonstrated within the piece itself, for these problems are soluble only beyond the confines of the stage. *The Sisters* is about loneliness, and the suffocating, cobwebby texture of decaying dreams, but it is also about theatre. If any way forward is to be found for the sisters it will take place there. *Goliath*, by contrast, is about economic deprivation, and it finally relocates this problem, from the stage, to the real world and the actual entities that must eventually find its solution: the forces of government and the community at large.

BIBLIOGRAPHY

Angier, C. (1990) *Jean Rhys: Life and Work*, London: André Deutsch.
Campbell, B. (1993) *Goliath*, London: Methuen.
Chekhov, A. (1959) *Plays*, trans. E. Fen, Harmondsworth: Penguin.
Chekhov, A. (1967) *The Oxford Chekhov, Volume II*, trans. and ed. R. Hingley, London, New York, Toronto: Oxford University Press.
Chekhov, A. (1964) *The Oxford Chekhov, Volume III*, trans. and ed. R. Hingley, London, New York, Toronto: Oxford University Press.
Fairweather, E., McDonough, R., & McFadyean, M. (1984) *Only the Rivers Run Free: Northern Ireland: The Women's War*, London: Pluto.
Fraser, A. (1988) *Boadicea's Chariot: The Warrior Queens*, London: Weidenfeld & Nicolson.
Lavery, B. (1997) *Goliath*, London: Methuen (Production Script).
Lavery, B. *More Light*, in (1997) *New Connections: New Plays for Young People*, London: Faber and Faber.
Marder, E. (1992) 'Disarticulated Voices: Feminism and Philomela', *Hypatia* 7, 2:148-66.
Rhys, J. (1969) (André Deutsch 1967) *Voyage in the Dark*, Harmondsworth: Penguin.
Spong, J.S. (1992) *Born of a Woman: A Bishop Rethinks the Birth of Christ*, San Francisco: Harper.
Styan, J.L. (1971) *Chekhov in Performance: A Commentary on the Major Plays*, Cambridge: Cambridge University Press.

Unpublished play scripts

Boadicea: The Red-Bellied Queen, Foursight Theatre (stimulus script by Cath Kilcoyne)
Goliath, Bryony Lavery (pre-Bush-Theatre version)
Paper Walls, text by Cindy Oswin, with contributions by the original performers
Slap, Naomi Cooke and Kate Hale
The Sisters, adaptation by Andrzej Sadowski
Voyage in the Dark, adaptation by Joan Wiles

INDEX

Anderson, Helen, 30-2

Belt and Braces, 104
Berman, Ed, 104
Bernard, Emma, 32
Byrne, Gráinne, 5, 29–30, 32–3, 37–8

Campbell, Beatrix, 2, 103, 149, 150
Castledine, Annie, 104, 149, 150, 151, 152, 153
Chekhov, Anton, 1, 8, 10, 159
Corness, Jeff, 78–9
Cooke, Naomi, 85, 92–8

Deavere Smith, Anna, 149, 150
Deszcz, Katarzyna, 5, 8–9, 11, 27–8, 29, 31, 32

Foursight Theatre, 1, 2, 160

Glass Ceiling conferences, 103–4

Hale, Kate, 54, 59, 75–7, 79, 81, 85, 92–8

IOU Theatre, 79, 80

Jacob, Stephanie, 79, 80–1

Kagan, Jenny, 131
Kerr Scott, Linda, 33
Kilcoyne, Cath, 57, 59, 75–7, 78, 80, 81

Lavery, Bryony, 149–54
  More Light, 153–4

McAuliffe, Nichola, 150, 151, 152, 154
McIntyre, Clare, 104
Mandala Theatre, 4, 5
Might and Main Productions, 79
Mishima, Yukio, 108

Oswin, Cindy, 49

Parrish, Sue, 1, 103, 104–5, 107–10, 132
Pendlebury, Sue, 54, 75, 76, 80, 81
Pinnock, Winsome, 104
Piper, Nigel, 49
Power, Alice, 46–50
Punch and Judies, 104
Purcell, Alice, 46, 48, 49

Ratcliff, Katharine, 79, 80, 81
Red Ladder, 104
Rhys, Jean, 2, 108, 109, 110, 129, 130, 131, 132, 158
  Good Morning Midnight, 130
  Quartet, 129, 130
  Smile Please, 129
  Tigers are Better Looking, 129
  Wide Sargasso Sea, 130
Ribchester, Kerry, 76, 77–8

Sadowski, Andrzej, 1, 5, 8, 9, 11, 28, 29
Scarlet Harlets, 1, 4

Scarlet Theatre, 1, 2, 3, 160
Sphinx Theatre (The), 1, 2, 158
Stanislavski, Constantin, 10
   Stanislavskian exercises, 14, 16, 23

Thorp, Simon, 79–80

Ullyart, Kendra, 150, 151

Volcano Theatre, 79

Wertenbaker, Timberlake, 104
Wilcken, Franziska, 131
Wilde Players (The), 79
Wiles, Joan, 129–32
Women's Company (The), 104
Women's Theatre Group (The), 1, 103, 104

Other titles in the Contemporary Theatre Studies series:

Volume 17
Feminist Stages: Interviews with Women in Contemporary British Theatre
Lizbeth Goodman
Research Assistant: Jane de Gay

Volume 18
Public Selves, Political Stages: Interviews with Icelandic Women in Government and Theatre
Leigh Woods and Ágústa Gunnarsdóttir

Volume 19
Howard Barker's Theatre of Seduction
Charles Lamb

Volume 20
Augustine (Big Hysteria)
Anna Furse.
With a foreword by Elaine Showalter

Volume 21
Yury Lyubimov at the Taganka Theatre 1964–1994
Birgit Beumers

Volume 22
Gardzienice: Polish Theatre in Transition
Paul Allain

Volume 23
Beyond the Echoes of Soweto.
Five Plays by Matsemela Manaka
Edited by Geoffrey V. Davis

Volume 24
David Rudkin: Sacred Disobedience. An Expository Study of his Drama 1954–96
David Ian Rabey

Volume 25
Rescuers Speaking
A play by Wilfred Harrison

Volume 26
The Arab in Israeli Drama and Theatre
Dan Urian

Volume 27
Peter Brook: Oxford to Orghast
Richard Helfer and Glenn Loney

Volume 28
Edward Gordon Craig:
A Vision of the Theatre
Christopher Innes

Volume 29
Edward Bond Letters: Volume 4
Selected and edited by Ian Stuart

Volume 30
The Mask: A Periodical Performance by Edward Gordon Craig
Olga Taxidou

Volume 31
The Judaic Nature of Israeli Theatre:
A Search for Identity
Dan Urian. Translated by Naomi Paz

Volume 32
The Analysis of Performance Art:
A Guide to its Theory and Practice
Anthony Howell

Volume 33
The German Volksbühne Movement:
A History
Cecil Davies

Volume 34
Recording Women: A Documentation of Six Theatre Productions
Geraldine Cousin

This book is part of a series. The publisher will accept continuation orders which may be cancelled at any time and which provide for automatic billing and shipping of each title in the series upon publication. Please write for details.

For Product Safety Concerns and Information please contact our EU
representative GPSR@taylorandfrancis.com
Taylor & Francis Verlag GmbH, Kaufingerstraße 24, 80331 München, Germany